The Cloning Issue

ISSUES

Volume 12

Editor

Craig Donnellan

Independence

Educational Publishers
Cambridge

First published by Independence
PO Box 295
Cambridge CB1 3XP
England

British Library Cataloguing in Publication Data
The Cloning Issue – (Issues Series)
I. Donnellan, Craig II. Series
660.6'5

ISBN 1 86168 190 9

Printed in Great Britain
The Burlington Press
Cambridge

Typeset by
Claire Boyd

Cover
The illustration on the front cover is by
Pumpkin House.

CONTENTS

Introduction

The Cloning Issue is the twelfth volume in the Issues series. The aim of this series is to offer up-to-date information about important issues in our world.

The Cloning Issue examines the issues of human and animal cloning.

The information comes from a wide variety of sources and includes:
Government reports and statistics
Newspaper reports and features
Magazine articles and surveys
Literature from lobby groups
and charitable organisations.

It is hoped that, as you read about the many aspects of the issues explored in this book, you will critically evaluate the information presented. It is important that you decide whether you are being presented with facts or opinions. Does the writer give a biased or an unbiased report? If an opinion is being expressed, do you agree with the writer?

The Cloning Issue offers a useful starting-point for those who need convenient access to information about the many issues involved. However, it is only a starting-point. At the back of the book is a list of organisations which you may want to contact for further information.

*****

Human cloning

Global debates about human cloning are raging following claims that experiments are set to start. Jane Perrone explains the issue

What is cloning?

The Human Genetics Advisory Commission has defined cloning as 'producing a cell or organism with the same nuclear genome as another cell or organism'.

What about cloning humans?

Scientists began cloning frogs in the 1950s. When a team from the Roslin Institute in Edinburgh successfully cloned an adult mammal for the first time in 1996, the possibility of human cloning came a step closer to reality. No one has managed to clone a human being yet, but several groups have announced that they plan to do so.

How is it done?

Dolly the sheep was cloned by transferring the nucleus of a body cell into an egg which had already had its nucleus removed. This is also known as nuclear transfer. It is likely that an attempt to clone humans would be based on the same method.

Why do it?

A supply of donor organs, eradicating genetic diseases and allowing infertile couples to reproduce are some of the more mainstream reasons to clone humans. Then there are the more outlandish reasons for cloning, including cloning dead people and seeking eternal life by cloning as old age approaches.

Why is the National Academy of Sciences discussing cloning?

The ongoing debate about the ethical, medical, social and scientific implications of human cloning is growing as more scientists announce plans to clone humans. The academy is gathering information from leading scientists in the field before it puts together a report on whether the US should impose a moratorium on human cloning.

Which scientists will be there?

The session likely to provoke the most media interest will discuss human cloning. The three speakers – Severino Antinori, the head of a thriving Rome-based chain of IVF clinics, Panayiotis Michael Zavos, who heads an organisation called The Andrology Institute, and Brigitte Boisselier of Clonaid, which sells itself as 'the first human cloning company' – have all said they are planning human cloning experiments.

Antinori and Zavos claim that they have the volunteers and the funding to begin human cloning trials in November.

Clonaid, which was set up by a UFO-worshipping cult called the Raelians, says it plans to beat them in the race to produce the first human clone.

Is human cloning legal?

The Food and Drug Administration has prohibited human cloning in the US, and the House of Representatives has voted to ban human cloning for any purpose. George Bush is considering whether to allow use of government funds in embryonic stem cell research, including such research that does not involve cloning.

In Britain, Alan Milburn, the health secretary, announced in April that the UK will ban human cloning in a bid to lay to rest the 'twin spectres' of human cloning and a 'genetic underclass'.

What is stem cell research?

Stem cells are the master cells found in early stage embryos. They evolve into all the different tissues of the body, and doctors hope to treat many diseases by directing the cells to develop into needed implants.

At present, scientists usually obtain them from human embryos discarded during fertility treatments. However, human cloning techniques could create a continuous supply of stem cells for such research.

Why ban human cloning?

Most mainstream scientists are set against attempts at reproductive human cloning, including Ian Wilmut, the British embryologist who led the team which cloned Dolly the sheep, and Richard Gardner, who chaired a Royal Society working group on human cloning. The most persuasive argument is that the risks are far too great at present. It is feared that human cloning would be cruel, because the process may result in a large number of miscarriages and deformities before a human could be successfully cloned. For instance, it took 272 attempts to create Dolly. Even then, the child could not be guaranteed ongoing good health.

As Prof Gardner put it: 'Our experience with animals suggests that there would be a very real danger of creating seriously handicapped individuals if anybody tries to implant cloned human embryos into the womb.'

Many religious groups, including some Roman Catholic and Muslim organisations, also object to cloning. There are many ethical arguments for a ban, including fears that cloning humans will lead to 'designer babies' with genetic traits selected by their parents, or a black market for embryos, and the creation of a 'genetic underclass'.

© Guardian Newspapers Limited 2001

Cloning timeline

Information from LIFE

<300BC
Greek word *klon* used for twigs employed in vegetative reproduction of plants.

1932
Brave New World by Aldous Huxley published, bringing the idea of manufactured human life to a mass audience.

1966
Nuclear Transfer (same technology as Dolly) successfully performed in frogs by Gurdon.

July 1978
Louise Brown, the world's first test-tube baby, born. IVF worked upon by numerous fertility experts around the world, and although success rates are still low, around 8,000 babies are born every year in UK by IVF.

1990
Human Fertilisation and Embryology (HFE) Act introduced allowing the deliberate creation and experimentation upon human embryos for up to 14 days after fertilisation.

5 July 1996
Dolly the sheep, the first clone of an adult mammal, born.

23 February 1997
Scientists at the Roslin Institute in Scotland announce the birth of Dolly.

2 January 1998
A government committee releases *A Consultation Document on Human Cloning*, detailing many benefits of 'full pregnancy' cloning while largely ignoring moral issues.

6 November 1998
Scientists in America isolate and grow in the laboratory human embryonic stem cells for the first time.

16 August 2000
Chief Medical Officer Liam Donaldson releases report entitled *Stem Cell Research: Medical Progress with Responsibility*, advocating the introduction of 'therapeutic' cloning in the UK and the banning of 'full pregnancy' cloning. The Government immediately backs the proposals.

6 September 2000
Motion passed by European Parliament rejecting all forms of cloning.

19 December 2000 & 22 January 2001
House of Commons (Dec) and House of Lords (Jan) vote to extend the 1990 HFE Act to allow 'therapeutic' cloning. Legal proceedings to check the validity of this new legislation have prevented anyone starting research (as of July 2001).

March 2001
Italian fertility expert Severino Antinori and American Panayiotis Zavos announce that they are to begin work cloning humans beings so that infertile couples may have children. Their announcement led to criticism from around the world. Professor Antinori thanked Tony Blair for passing the UK legislation, which he said would help his work.

© LIFE

Human cloning

Information from the Christian Institute

CHRISTIAN INFLUENCE IN A SECULAR WORLD

What is cloning?

- Cloning involves the creation of an embryo which is an identical copy of another human being. Clones can be created through dividing an embryo at its earliest stage (creating two identical embryos). They can also be created using Cell Nuclear Replacement, the technique used to create Dolly the Sheep in 1997.

- In Cell Nuclear Replacement the nucleus of one cell is placed into an egg which has had its own nucleus removed. It is then stimulated to divide so that it becomes a clone.

- The Government has sought to make a distinction between 'therapeutic' and 'reproductive' cloning. However the process of creating a human life in embryo form is the same in either case.

Reproductive cloning

- In reproductive cloning the created embryo is implanted into a human womb, leading to the birth of a human being. Whilst this is now technically possible, it has never been done anywhere in the world. The Government has announced its intention to make 'reproductive' cloning specifically illegal.

Therapeutic cloning

- Therapeutic cloning also creates human beings in embryo form through cloning but the embryos are experimented upon and destroyed.

- 'Therapeutic cloning' has no therapeutic value for the subject involved. In fact it is literally lethal, necessarily bringing about the death of the embryo.

- On 19th December 2000 the House of Commons became the first legislature in the world to vote explicitly to legalise human cloning. The House of Lords confirmed this decision on 22nd January 2001. This was done not by primary legislation but by a Ministerial Order.

- Under the Order, Parliament has allowed for scientists to clone embryos for research.

Why do scientists want to clone embryos for research?

- 'Stem cells' are of great importance to research into curing human diseases. Stem cells are a unique kind of cell that can potentially develop into any other human cell. It is the need for these cells which is the background to the whole debate on cloning.

- Stem cells are found in human embryos and in human tissue such as bone marrow. Human embryos are very difficult to come by as it involves extracting female ova by an operation and then fertilising them.

- Scientists believe that stem cells will be useful in replacing cells

that have become diseased. Many claim that embryos provide the best source of these cells and that cloning is necessary to be able to create more embryos as a more readily available source of stem cells.

- However, taking stem cells from an embryo necessarily involves the destruction of the embryo. Currently the supply of embryos comes as a by-product of In-Vitro Fertilisation (IVF). The parents donate their excess embryos for the research.

- Parliament has allowed embryos to be cloned so that stem cells can be extracted for research. They have legalised human cloning. The Government is clear that this will be for research purposes, not to breed human beings by implanting cloned embryos into a womb. Until the Government brings in legislation to explicitly outlaw reproductive cloning, the Human Fertilisation and Embryology Authority (HFEA) will not license the practice.

Biblical arguments

Human cloning creates human beings – from conception

Whether it be 'therapeutic' or 'reproductive' cloning – both techniques create human life.

Life is sacred from conception. The embryo has personhood at conception regardless of how that conception comes about. Once a new life has been created through cloning there is no moral distinction between it and any other embryo. All embryos deserve our protection.

'Therapeutic' cloning is morally repugnant because it creates life with the specific aim of experimentation and destruction. The stem cells are extracted for research and the embryo dies. In the USA this practice has been called 'technological cannibalism' by one pro-life group.

'Reproductive' cloning is also morally indefensible on the following grounds:

Human cloning is biological manufacturing by man not creation by God
Human cloning, and particularly 'reproductive cloning', puts the choices about a new life in the hands of a person rather than God. It will be left to the scientist to decide which embryo appears fit for implantation and which should be discarded. Human cloning usurps God's position as the Almighty Creator. Job acknowledged, 'The Lord gave and the Lord has taken away' (Job 1:21).

Under this new regime man, and not God, chooses the desired characteristics of any resultant children. It gives man control over the next generation. Cloning gives humans control over human fertility and therefore over the design/genetics of future generations. Thus man exerts a tyranny over future generations. As C. S. Lewis said:

'In reality, of course, if any one age really attains, by eugenics and scientific education, the power to make its descendants what it pleases, all men who live after it are the patients of that power. They are

> *God's intention is that children are procreated using genetic material from both their parents. With cloning the genetic material comes from only one 'parent'*

weaker, not stronger: for though we may have put wonderful machines in their hands we have pre-ordained how they are to use them.'[1]

Children are a gift from God
Children are a gift from God.[2] No one has a 'right' to have children even though they may be earnestly desired and infertility is usually found to be deeply distressing.[3] However, cloning and many forms of in-vitro fertilisation (IVF) make commodities out of children who are 'made to order'. Procreation is taken out of God's hands and given to man.

Cloning breaks the link with parents
God created man and woman; he instituted marriage for their mutual benefit and for the procreation of children.[4] God told Adam and Eve

to 'Be fruitful and increase in number; fill the earth and subdue it.'[5]

In this way human relationships are based on relations between a husband and wife, their children and the wider family. God's creation of the marriage relationship, and its central place in the procreation of the next generation, is for our benefit.

God's intention is that children are procreated using genetic material from both their parents. With cloning the genetic material comes from only one 'parent'. The child will be the genetic brother of the 'father' or the genetic sister of the 'mother'. This profoundly undermines God's intended order for procreation.

References:
1 Lewis C S *The Abolition of Man*, Harper Collins Religious, 1978, page 35
2 Psalm 127:3 'Sons are a heritage from the Lord, children a reward from him'
3 1 Samuel chapter 1
4 Genesis 2:24 'For this reason a man will leave his father and mother and be united to his wife, and they will become one flesh'
5 Genesis 1:28

Public perspectives on human cloning

Information from the Wellcome Trust

Introduction
Public Perspectives on Human Cloning presents the results of a public consultation exercise, commissioned by the Wellcome Trust in the spring of 1998, on human cloning and the use of cloning technology in medical research. The aim of the research was to provide input from members of the public who do not usually have a voice in such issues (the 'uninvolved public') to the Human Genetics Advisory Commission (HGAC)/Human Fertilisation and Embryology Authority's

 The Wellcome Trust

(HFEA) joint consultation document, *Cloning Issues in Reproduction, Science and Medicine*. Preliminary findings were included in the Wellcome Trust's response to the Working Party.

The sample
Within the time available it was the Trust's intention to bring the views

of people not usually consulted in policy discussions about the social and ethical implications of biomedical research into the policy debate.

Ten focus groups and four paired depth interviews with opposite-sex couples were carried out, involving a total of 79 adults in three English cities and two locations in the south-east.

Four groups were chosen as a cross-section of society.[1] Quotas based on age, sex and whether or not they had children were used as proxies for interest in reproductive technology. Socio-economic group provided an indication of educational level. The highest and lowest social grades were excluded, firstly because of the time available and the known difficulty in recruiting these socio-economic groups to studies. Secondly, it was felt that those with limited education, of which social grade can be indicative, would find the stimulus material difficult to understand.

Other groups (lesbians, women who had lost a young child grandparents, pregnant women, women who had difficulty conceiving and women in their late 30s and early 40s with no children) were chosen because these groups might have different views from the 'mainstream' on human cloning for a number of reasons.

What participants thought about human cloning

Reproductive cloning, where an entire human is produced from a single cell by asexual reproduction, was regarded as unacceptable by virtually all participants. This was a widespread and often spontaneous reaction.

Opening discussions probed participants' general perceptions of medical and genetic research both spontaneously and also prompted by presenting several scientific terms on cards. References to cloning often pre-empted the formal introduction of the topic by the facilitator. A common theme was that participants closely associated cloning with the term 'genetic engineering'.

'I'm concerned with the idea of genetic engineering and cloning. There are big moral issues.'
Woman 30s/40s I[2]

'I think it's frightening [genetic engineering], particularly because of the sheep and how far it is going to go.'
Woman who had lost a child I

Many participants claimed to have a vivid image in their mind of what a clone would be. When prompted, responses commonly described 'photocopied' individuals and automated production lines or artificial incubators producing

multiple adult clones. This concept of human cloning was linked to its adoption by malevolent outside influences such as the military, megalomaniac leaders and rogue scientists. Examples frequently cited were genetic experiments conducted by the Nazis.

'Very disturbing – why would you want a replica of you? I certainly wouldn't. It reminds me of Hitler, trying to create a race.'
C2D man I

'You just think about Hitler, Aryan race.'
BC1 woman I

'I can just imagine all these people walking around looking the same.'
C2D woman I

Almost all participants continued to reject the idea of human cloning throughout the research, even after explanations of the science behind cloning and in-depth discussion about the influence of environmental factors, such as growing up in different eras.

Cultural references to cloning

Popular culture provided an important frame for reactions to human cloning.

'You see it on films, armies of marching robots. Why do we need cloning?'
Woman who had lost a child I

'I dread to think what could happen if it was to end up like something out of a sci-fi film.'
Grandparent, diary

Discussions were peppered throughout with negative references to films and books including *The Boys from Brazil, Jurassic Park, Blade Runner, Invasion of the Bodysnatchers, Frankenstein, Brave New World, Stepford Wives, Star Trek* and *Alien Resurrection*. These references were often used to punctuate discussion, but it was not always clear which aspects of the film were being alluded to. Classic stories such as *Frankenstein, Brave New World*, and, to a lesser extent, *The Boys from Brazil*, were not referred to in detail, but were often simply cited as examples. Just the reference to a film or book appeared to be sufficient to describe participants' concerns, and there was an assumption that others in the group would be able to understand these instantly. Several participants mentioned having seen the film *GATTACA*, which was on general release over the research period, but in cases where there was less familiarity they took more time to explain the general plot to others in the group.

'Cloning . . . I mean it's Frankenstein-type medicine.'
BC1 man I

'It's a Star Trek thing – androids with a brain that could think like a human.'
Woman 30s/40s I

'I have a Brave New World vision where we have half a dozen or so different kinds of human being classified according to their ability . . . I think Mr Huxley was quite perceptive.'

BC1 man I

Dissenting views

The proposal that several previously suggested groups might accept reproductive cloning was not supported by this research. There was no evidence, for example, that those who had lost a child or who might want to extend their own genetic existence, had more positive attitudes than others towards reproductive cloning.

Four individuals in two of the groups held a rather different view in that they thought that human cloning might be a *desirable* development. In each case, the dissenting views were expressed within a group where the majority were more negative towards human reproductive cloning. Each dissenting view appears distinct in its reasoning and these alternative viewpoints are of interest as they may also be held within important minority groups.

Cloning as 'progress'

Two men in the C2D[3] group contemplated the idea that human cloning might represent 'progress' and should therefore be accepted. In the reconvened group, one of the two men acknowledged that he still felt rather overwhelmed with the information provided. While he believed his knowledge might be incomplete, his judgement in approving human cloning was clear:

'I was trying to get my head round it but I could not see any bad points in it, you are able to do it . . . so therefore I think it would be a good thing.'

C2D man II

'In some ways it's the way forward, it is moving forward all the time.'

C2D man II

A second man in this group expressed excitement at the unknown possibilities that human cloning might offer and was reluctant

to proscribe further research in this area even if unforeseen or negative consequences might arise. He believed that such risks were acceptable and an integral part of 'the future'. This participant also questioned the distinction between artificial and natural processes.

'You know people say well it's wrong, we mustn't, it's dangerous. I don't think nature is a fixed thing. Who are we to say that it is nature and it begins there and it ends there . . . if you look at it as something open then you can experiment and I think all things, everything, started off as an experiment and everything probably went wrong. You know there is no way we can get it right first time, so whilst I find it very exciting – the whole thing – I strangely feel no fear about it.'

C2D man II

Social consequences of cloning

Many participants considered that a cloned child would face significant social problems that could affect their upbringing. How would a child respond to knowing that he/she was cloned rather than created through sexual reproduction? Would this not lead to the child becoming

'No amount of research could fully conclude the mental effects on a genetically identical person.'

Pregnant woman, diary

'The child doesn't know who it belongs to, or, family background, it's just, it's just not right!'

C2D woman II

stigmatised and discriminated against by others? Such questions seemed impossible to resolve.

Participants' emphasis was on whether an appropriate social environment could be offered for the upbringing of a child produced through cloning. Scenarios shown to participants depicting a single woman or two women having a cloned child raised greater concerns.

'I think the worst thing is like the woman, having a baby on her own. I can't imagine what you would feel like, growing up and being told that actually you did not have a father at all, genetically.'

C2D woman II

Is a unique genetic identity important?

Participants considered it highly selfish for an individual to want to create a genetic copy of themselves through cloning. However, initial concerns that human cloning would lead to a loss of individuality lessened somewhat over the research period. There was discussion of how identical twins would have the same genetic make-up and the role that genes might play in controlling their behaviour and personality.

'I can see that you would have a baby that looks like you, but they're not going to have your upbringing, and that's what makes a child – the way they're treated as a child.'

Women who had lost a child II

The teaching materials had illustrated to participants that human cloning would produce a child, not an identical adult, as many first believed. As the issue was discussed, several participants appeared to accept that a child brought up at a different time with different environmental influences would not have an identical personality to the original, despite having an identical genetic make-up.

This modified view of the influence of nurture over nature did not, however, undermine their fundamental rejection of human cloning.

'You could never recreate a person unless they have gone through the same experiences. It's not nurture it's nature. We're talking about character, personality, whatever it is one loves about someone. You're never going to reproduce that.'

Woman 30s/40s II

Notes
1 The classification is based on the Market Research Society's grade groupings. Across all ages, Groups B, C1, C2 and D cover approximately 84 per cent of the population. Groups BC1 approximate to non-manual occupations and Groups CSD to manual occupations. Group A, 3 per cent of the population (professionals, very senior managers and top-level civil servants) and Group E, 13 per cent (those who are long-term dependent on the state, whether through sickness, unemployment, old age or other reasons) were not included in this sample.
2 'I' after a quote indicates a participant in one of the first discussions. Figure 'II' indicates a participant in a reconvened group. 'Diary' refers to the diaries kept by participants between the initial and reconvened groups.
3 This occupational grouping includes skilled and unskilled manual workers.

• The above information is an extract from *Public Perspectives on Human Cloning*, produced by the Wellcome Trust. See page 41 for their address details.

© The Wellcome Trust

Cloning: disaster or necessity?

As peers threaten to block government plans to allow the cloning of embryos, science editor Tim Radford looks at a medical revolution

DNA has been around for 3.8bn years, renewing itself with each life at conception. In humans, a length of adult DNA from a male enters an egg and unites with DNA from a female, turns back the clock, becomes the first infant cell, divides and starts a cascade of reactions that turns one fertilised egg into 1,000bn cells of more than 200 different kinds.

How it does this is a whole series of mysteries, but one key to these lies in first stem cells from which all bone, skin, blood and nerves subsequently stem. These appear in the first 14 days, before the cell implants in the womb.

For the last 10 years, British scientists have used embryos up to 14 days old to assist infertile couples to a pregnancy, and to study the puzzles of infertility.

Four years ago, Scottish scientists stunned the world by taking DNA from a dead sheep and growing Dolly. Then three years ago, US scientists working with private money managed to 'immortalise' stem cells in a laboratory dish.

The combination of the two discoveries seemed to open a magic door: onto a horizon in which incurable, irreversible diseases such as multiple sclerosis and Parkinson's disease could one day be cured. 'Personalised' stem cells could be grown in a dish, and implanted in a

By Tim Radford

sufferer, to make new nerve cells grow. The paralysed *Superman* actor, Christopher Reeve, might walk again.

American federal law will not permit taxpayers' money to finance embryo research of any kind, but US private laboratories can do what they like.

For the last 10 years, British scientists have used embryos up to 14 days old to assist infertile couples to a pregnancy, and to study the puzzles of infertility

In Britain, all such research is subject to the Human Fertilisation and Embryology Act. A government committee considered the opening, and gave the green light to a very limited extension to permit research into embryos up to 14 days old for other diseases besides those of infertility.

Nervously, the government created another committee, which also gave the green light. Again nervously, the government then permitted a free vote in the House of Commons. It passed, by a huge majority.

Now, driven by some, but not all, religious groups, the House of Lords could kick the legislation into touch, or at least into the next parliament, by referring 'therapeutic cloning' to a committee.

Dissidents argue that latest experiments with 'adult' stem cells mean that embryos may need never to be used. There is a case: there could never be enough donated eggs to make the stem cells that doctors would ultimately need.

The hope is that ultimately stem cells from adults could be 'reprogrammed' to cure diseases. But at present, the only way to get to that point is to study stem cells as they emerge in the first 14 days, using surplus embryos that would otherwise be destroyed.

The Roman Catholic Church and other groups talk of embryo stem cell research as a 'dehumanising' and disastrous step. That's not how Parkinson's disease and muscular dystrophy campaign groups see it, nor the British Medical Association, nor the Imperial Cancer Research Fund, nor Diabetes UK.

© Guardian Newspapers Limited 2001

Cloning

Information from the Centre for Bioethics and Public Policy (CBPP)

What is cloning?

It is the production of an individual identical to another. The first mammal to be cloned was Dolly, the sheep, born in 1997. She was created by scientists at the Roslin Institute in Edinburgh. This was by means of a revolutionary technique.

An unfertilised egg was taken from an adult sheep and its nucleus was removed, only to be replaced by the nucleus from an adult sheep cell, a mammalian cell from another sheep. Not only was it remarkable that an egg emptied of its nucleus would accept another nucleus from a foreign adult cell, but more remarkable still was it that the egg with its new nucleus should act as an embryo.

So why did it act as an embryo? This was for two reasons. First, the cell behaved like a fertilised egg, because – unlike an unfertilised egg – it contained a double set of chromosomes, just like an ordinary embryo. What happens at fertilisation is that an egg with a single set of chromosomes fuses with a sperm with a single set of chromosomes, to form an embryo, with a double set of chromosomes, one set from the mother and one set from the father. The embryo then grows by cell division. And each new cell has a double set of chromosomes. This means that virtually all the cells in the body have a double set of chromosomes – one set from the mother and one set from the father. The big exceptions are the gametes, the eggs in the woman's body and the sperms in the man's body. So to reiterate, one reason why the egg used to create Dolly behaved as an embryo when its nucleus was replaced with the nucleus from an adult cell was that it contained a double set of chromosomes, one set from a male and one set from a female.

The other reason why the egg-cell used to create Dolly behaved as an embryo was that the scientists managed to bring it back to a toti-potent state. This means that it was

able to develop into different kinds of cell, just like an ordinary embryo. This was remarkable, because most of the cells in our bodies are not of this kind. For when the embryo develops and the cells differentiate into different types, certain genes in the cells are turned off. Thus in skin cells certain genes only are turned on, all the others are turned off. In muscle cells other genes only are turned on. By contrast, in toti-potent cells all the genes are turned on. The fact that the cell used to create Dolly was returned to the toti-potent state was the second reason why it behaved as an embryo.

Human reproductive cloning

Human reproductive cloning in order to create human beings is considered unethical by most scientists, ethicists and politicians. When the House of Lords last spring voted on human cloning they ruled out human reproductive cloning, but not stem cell research involving the use of human embryos. Likewise the Council of Europe and the ethics groups advising the European Commission have called for a total ban on human reproductive cloning.

The reasons for rejecting human reproductive cloning are the follow-

ing. It is considered an offence against human dignity, because it would fail to respect the uniqueness of each one of us and involve the manufacture of children as copies of others already in existence. It is pointed out that even identical twins are unique in the sense of being unpredictable gifts of God or nature. As the Chief Rabbi, Jonathan Sacks, wrote in *The Times* (09/08/01), 'every child born of the genetic mix between two parents is unpredictable, a gift of grace, like-yet-unlike those who have brought it into the world'. In short, the objection to human reproductive cloning is twofold. First, it means treating human beings as products and, secondly, it means creating them as replicas of others.

Stem-cell research

Stem cells are precursors of differentiated cells, such as skin cells, blood cells, muscle cells and nerve cells. They are toti-potent or pluri-potent. Toti-potent cells, such as embryonic cells, are capable of developing into any type of cell. Pluri-potent stem cells are slightly less versatile, that is to say, they can develop into a number of different kinds of cell but perhaps not all kinds. Adult stem cells, such as can be found in the bone marrow, for example, are thought to be pluri-potent rather than toti-potent.

The reason why the House of Lords voted in favour of stem-cell research involving the creation of human embryos was the belief that embryonic stem cells might be more useful for therapeutic purposes than adult stem cells. The aim is to seek cures for neural diseases such as Parkinson's disease and Alzheimer's; and it is hoped that stems could be used for this purpose. Stem cells might also be used to renew the skin of people who have burnt themselves badly. Alternatively, they might be used to repair damaged muscle tissue.

However, there are many who object to the use of embryonic stem cells. This is on the ground that the human embryo is a human being in the making, who deserves our respect. In order to use embryonic stem cells it would be necessary either to remove stem cells from embryos left over after fertility treatment or to create and destroy embryos specifically in order to harvest their stem cells. The embryonic stem cells are the inner cells in the developing embryo. The outer cells are slightly differentiated in order to become the placenta and other supportive tissue. Those who object to the use of embryonic stem cells regard it as a form of cannibalising the embryo.

While not necessarily objecting strongly to embryonic stem-cell research on moral grounds, there are

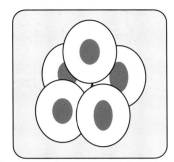

also those who point out that it might be unnecessary. This is because recent research has found that adult stem cells are, in fact, capable of developing into different kinds of tissue. For example, pluri-potent blood stem cells may be transformed into neural stem cells and, hence, into neural cells for neural cell repair. The ethics group advising the

European Commission and the European Parliament are advocating research with adult stem cells so as to avoid the use of human embryos.

In the United States President Bush has just declared that embryonic stem cell research may only be undertaken using existing embryonic stem cell lines. No new embryos are to be created or used for this purpose. In Britain the legal situation is unclear at present. This is because the ProLife Alliance has been granted a judicial review of present legislation governing embryo research. The date for this review is 31st October 2001. The review may result in an overhaul of the law as it stands.

© *Centre for Bioethics and Public Policy (CBPP)*

Birth of a miracle

Soon you may not need eggs or sperm to have children of your own

Men and women who can't produce sperm or eggs could one day have 'natural' children of their own thanks to a form of cloning.

Gianpiero Palermo of Cornell University in New York has created artificial human eggs that contain just one set of a would-be mother's chromosomes. Such eggs could be fertilised with the partner's sperm, just like a normal egg.

And in Australia, Orly Lacham-Kaplan of Monash University in Melbourne has shown that you can fertilise eggs, not with sperm, but with cells taken from elsewhere in the body. But there are still considerable obstacles to overcome before either technique could be used to create human babies.

The trouble is that we inherit not just genes, but chemical marks, or imprints, that turn some genes off. Chromosomes taken from body cells have different patterns of imprinting to egg and sperm cells, and that could cause developmental abnormalities. This may be why some clones have problems.

Because of the risks, adds Palermo, careful testing in animals and further understanding of

By Claire Ainsworth

imprinting works are needed before the new methods are applied to humans. 'It's something we are evaluating,' he says. 'We're just going one step at a time.'

Although existing fertility treatments can help men with low sperm counts, they don't work for men who make abnormal sperm, or no sperm at all

If the technique can be made safe, it would help the growing number of people who can conceive only with the help of donated eggs or sperm – and are therefore not genetically related to their children. Some women lose their eggs because of chemotherapy or ovarian surgery. But many women are also finding themselves in this situation because

they've put off childbirth until it's too late. And although existing fertility treatments can help men with low sperm counts, they don't work for men who make abnormal sperm, or no sperm at all.

One solution would be cloning: transplanting genetic material from, say, a skin cell of the would-be mother or father into an egg from which the DNA has been removed. But because the baby would be identical to its parent, this technique is highly controversial and likely to be banned in many countries.

So Palermo and his colleagues are trying to use cloning techniques to create eggs that behave more as nature intended. Like normal cells in our body, a mature human egg usually has two sets of chromosomes – one inherited from the woman's mother, the other from her father. When the egg is fertilised, it retains one set in a so-called pronucleus, and spits out the rest in a little package called the polar body. The fertilising sperm, which contains just one set of chromosomes, then restores the full complement.

Palermo's team has mimicked this process by transplanting a nucleus from a body cell into a mature human egg that has had its genetic material removed. By prodding the reconstituted egg with a pulse of electricity, they can make the nucleus divide in half, forming two pronuclei. The team removes one pronucleus and then fertilises the egg by injecting a sperm.

So far, however, the resulting embryos have stopped developing after only one or two rounds of cell division, they told a conference on human reproduction in Switzerland this week. 'This is preliminary work,' cautions Palermo, 'but at least in theory, it might be a way to provide eggs for sterile women.' However, a child created this way would inherit the DNA-containing structures called mitochondria from the donor egg, and would thus effectively have three parents (see *New Scientist*, 12 May 2001, p. 7).

Meanwhile, a related technique being developed by Lacham-Kaplan and her colleagues might help infertile men. The team has

succeeded in 'fertilising' a normal mouse egg using a cell taken from the body of a male. This is surprising, because the body cell has two sets of chromosomes.

But the team found that when the egg is exposed to certain chemicals, it spits out two polar bodies. One, as normal, contains the egg's spare chromosomes. But the other contains half the chromosomes of the transplanted nucleus, leaving the fertilised egg with the usual two sets.

Even more surprising, such eggs go on to develop relatively normally in the lab, up to the pre-implantation stage. Lacham-Kaplan is now trying to transfer these embryos into surrogate mice.

• From *New Scientist* 7 July 2001.

Team prepares to clone human being

Fertility experts present plans as last frontier in battle to defeat male sterility

It is a contest they are unlikely to win, and one many believe should not be waged. But amid the chaos and doubt in Rome yesterday, it was clear, at least, that Severino Antinori and his partners had fired the starting gun in a race to produce a cloned human being.

Boasting of unlimited funds, a choice of six countries to work in and an embarrassment of scientific expertise, the Antinori private human cloning consortium set out its stall at a seminar in Rome's Institute of Clinical Obstetrics and Gynaecology.

Or to put it another way, the consortium would not say where, when or how they would clone a human being, who would do it or how much it would cost.

Only the fact that Mr Antinori and his colleagues work with human embryos on a daily basis in their

By James Meek, Science Correspondent

fertility clinics and their single-minded determination to use cloning to treat one straightforward problem – male infertility – prompted the thought: What if they pulled it off?

Mr Antinori told the seminar – 90% of the delegates were, in fact, journalists – that his clinics had already begun sounding out clients.

Of 300 male patients whose sperm was unsuitable to produce children, he said, 70% had asked to be given the opportunity to produce a cloned child.

'Cloning may be the last frontier in our attempts to defeat male sterility,' he said. 'Cloning creates ordinary children who grow up to be unique individuals. We are here to encourage fruitful scientific research and good ethical behaviour.'

'We do intend to clone the first human being,' said Panos Zavos, Mr Antinori's key partner, who runs a fertility clinic in Lexington, Kentucky. 'This is a solution to a human problem.

'We want to do it as soon as possible, but we have no intention of stepping over dead bodies.'

Later he said the first experiments to lay the groundwork for the cloning programme could begin within weeks, with the first cloned embryo ready for implantation in a mother's womb within one and a half to two years.

He ruled out using the technology to try to clone dead children or famous people. The idea was to help men who had no sperm to have genetically related children without relying on a sperm donor.

'It's a dead-end street, it's a stop sign, if you're one of those males that face this particular difficulty, you think: "God, why me? Why do I have to borrow sperm in order to get a child?"' he said.

Mr Zavos added that, unlike animal cloning programmes, they would not be implanting scores of embryos in many surrogate mothers in the hope of getting one successful pregnancy.

Twenty-three years of human IVF work had laid the basis for a more sophisticated approach, he said, involving screening embryos at the stage when they consisted of only a few cells to select the most likely to implant successfully, cultivating extra embryos from the best, and then implanting them in one mother.

The appearance of a third partner on the platform, Avi Ben Abraham, described as an Israeli-American biotechnologist, prompted speculation that the 'Mediterranean country' referred to as a possible site for the first human cloning attempt was Israel. But the consortium would not be drawn.

If the organisation of yesterday's seminar was anything to go by, would-be clonees would be advised to look elsewhere. In the cramped well of a dingy lecture theatre, the animated, silver-haired Mr Antinori and assistants beat off waves of camera crews and photographers as they made their presentations.

At one point a man in a white coat entered and announced that the head of the department which ran the lecture theatre had been watching the seminar with mounting horror on CNN during a trip to China and strongly objected to an event supporting human cloning – condemned by the UN, the EU, the Council of Europe, the World Health Organisation and a catalogue of other bodies.

Towards the end, the hulking, bearded figure of Richard Seed, an early, discredited prophet of human cloning, unexpectedly took the floor. His last words before his microphone was cut off and he was led away were: 'I'm going to try to clone my wife first. I'm going to try to keep the first five clones in the family –'

Real cloning is seen as lying in the realms of science. For now, it does. But the equipment and know-how required to attempt to clone a human being is cheap and simple compared to that needed for a nuclear weapon or to put an astronaut in space.

Reproductive human cloning is not technically illegal in Britain, but the Human Fertilisation and Embryology Authority would certainly refuse permission. However, while some US states and countries, such as Japan, have banned it outright, others have not, and there are now few parts of the world without IVF centres: China, India and the former Soviet Union have many.

The science of human cloning is much tougher. All labs which have succeeded in cloning animals report a massive failure rate, from embryos failing to implant in wombs to miscarriages and deformities at birth.

The only lab in the world to have successfully cloned an animal from the family to which humans belong, the primates, told the *Guardian* this week that it had given up further attempts until it understood what was going wrong.

The Oregon Regional Primate Centre, which recently announced the birth of ANDi, the world's first genetically modified monkey, has never managed to clone a monkey using the Dolly technique, where an embryo is cultured from an adult cell. It has only ever done it with an older method, using a single cell from a natural embryo.

The centre's Don Wolf said: 'I think it's ridiculous to venture into the realm of human reproductive cloning. The risks are clearly unacceptable.'

Human cloning

Frequently asked questions. Information from the ProLife Alliance

Q. *What is cloning?*
A. An unfertilised ovum has its nucleus replaced by the nucleus of an adult cell. The resulting embryo is a twin of the donor of the nucleus and has identical DNA.

Q. *Is the ProLife Alliance against human cloning?*
A. Yes, we are totally opposed to the cloning of human beings, either with the intention of producing a live baby, or with the intention of taking cells from the clone embryo, who dies in the process (so-called 'therapeutic' cloning). Both kinds of cloning would involve using human embryos for experimentation. There are many other objections to each kind of cloning.

Q. *Why are you against 'therapeutic' cloning?*
A. The suggestion that a human should be created, grown for some days, and then harvested for spare parts, is a gross assault on human dignity. Of course there is no objection to the cultivation of for example someone's skin cells for his own benefit, but to create what is in effect a tiny twin sibling simply to be used, is very wrong. The new life is that of a real human being, as human as you or I are now, or were at that stage of our lives.

Q. *Why are you against cloning for birth/where the clone will be born?*
A. There are several drawbacks, apart from the destruction of human embryos which would necessarily happen during prior experimentation. The process is very risky. Many deformed lambs were produced in the making of Dolly the cloned sheep. Cloning would confuse family relationships harmfully, the baby being genetically the sibling of the DNA donor. It is a further step in the direction of 'commodification', of treating a baby as a commodity, a thing to be made to order and rejected if not as planned, rather than as an equal human being.

Cloned babies

The height of irresponsibility

By Dr Donald Bruce

The proposal by an Italian scientist to attempt to produce cloned human babies would be the height of irresponsibility were it allowed to take place. It gives science a bad name. It goes against established legal, ethical and medical understanding.

The practice has already been outlawed by the European Convention on Human Rights and Biomedicine, covering not just the EU but all European states. The fact that the scientist is having to go 'offshore' is testimony to the degree to which the practice is regarded as professionally, medically and ethically unacceptable.

Ethically there is a widespread international understanding that to clone a human being is wrong. To clone is to exercise an unprecedented control over someone else's complete genetic makeup. It is quite different from the randomness of identical twinning, where an embryo of unique and so far unknown genetic type spontaneously divides. Cloning takes the genetic material of an existing person and uses it as the basis of a new person. This does not mean an identical person, of course. All the other aspects we call 'environmental' factors will be different. For the first time a person would come into the world who had had their genes preordained by someone else. We argue that this is intrinsically wrong. We can reject our upbringing, education and social influences, but we cannot change our genes.

Equally important, it would be unthinkable in terms of medical risk. In 1998 the Farm Animal Welfare Council of the UK Ministry of Agriculture called for a moratorium on commercial uses of animal cloning, because of the serious welfare problems encountered when several animal species have been cloned. In such a context it would be criminally irresponsible to attempt a technique on humans which is known frequently to cause deformities, large foetuses and premature deaths in sheep and cattle. This departs from any medical justification.

Childlessness afflicts many couples, my wife and I included. Technologies like IVF have given many possibilities for helping the situation. But there are limits on how far the desire to be a parent justifies grabbing any form of technology in order to meet our desires. A good life is still possible without children, after all. As things currently stand the chances for any couple contemplating offering themselves would be more likely to produce deformed babies, miscarriages and early deaths than a healthy baby. No desire for a child is worth such terrible odds.

• Dr Bruce is Director of the Church of Scotland Society, Religion and Technology Project, assessing ethical issues in technology for Scotland's national church. He has been involved with the ethics of cloning since 1996 and is a leading authority on the subject. He is co-editor of the book *Engineering Genesis*.

Stars are offered way to stop fans cloning them

By Robert Uhlig, Technology Correspondent

A Californian company is offering celebrities the opportunity to copyright their DNA as a precaution against fans cloning them. In theory, all that is needed for someone to clone their hero or heroine is a few living cells left behind on a glass or exchanged in a handshake.

For high-profile celebrities worried that they might fall victim to cloners even after their death, the DNA Copyright Institute of San Francisco, or DCI, is offering to record their DNA fingerprint, check that it is unique and store it.

Andre Crump, president of DCI, said: 'A lot of people are going to want to clone people they admire.' As the pattern's 'author', the client would have copyright protection to prevent 'actions such as DNA theft and misappropriation, cloning and other unauthorised activities', he added.

According to Mr Crump, 10 people have already made use of the £1,000 service which includes a personalised plaque. 'Our type of clients will want something to hang on the wall and look good,' he said.

However, lawyers dismissed claims that DNA could be copyrighted. 'This is nonsense,' said Stephen Barnett of the University of California, Berkeley. 'Whoever is saying that is ignorant of the term copyright.'

Nevertheless, DCI maintained that its service was legally valid. Matthew Marca, the company's legal counsel, said since clones would share the fingerprint of the original person, they would be in violation of copyright.

A report in *New Scientist* pointed out that clones were not exact copies but often contained a new genetic component, namely DNA from the egg used to create an embryo.

The magazine reported: 'Mr Marca seemed taken aback when this was pointed out. After a pause, he responded confidently: "That is some of what will emerge in the eventual prosecution of DNA copyright."'

The benefits of human cloning

There are many ways in which human cloning is expected to benefit mankind. Below is a list that is far from complete. By Simon Smith

Rejuvenation

Dr Richard Seed, one of the leading proponents of human cloning technology, suggests that it may someday be possible to reverse the ageing process because of what we learn from cloning.

Human cloning technology could be used to reverse heart attacks

Scientists believe that they may be able to treat heart attack victims by cloning their healthy heart cells and injecting them into the areas of the heart that have been damaged. Heart disease is the number one killer in the United States and several other industrialised countries.

There has been a breakthrough with human stem cells

Embryonic stem cells can be grown to produce organs or tissues to repair or replace damaged ones. Skin for burn victims, brain cells for the brain damaged, spinal cord cells for quadriplegics and paraplegics, hearts, lungs, livers, and kidneys could be produced. By combining this technology with human cloning technology it may be possible to produce needed tissue for suffering people that will be free of rejection by their immune systems. Conditions such as Alzheimer's disease, Parkinson's disease, diabetes, heart failure, degenerative joint disease, and other problems may be made curable if human cloning and its technology are not banned.

Infertility

With cloning, infertile couples could have children. Despite getting a fair amount of publicity in the news current treatments for infertility, in terms of percentages, are not very successful. One estimate is that current infertility treatments are less than 10 per cent successful. Couples go through physically and emotionally painful procedures for a small chance of having children.

Many couples run out of time and money without successfully having children. Human cloning could make it possible for many more infertile couples to have children than ever before possible.

Plastic, reconstructive, and cosmetic surgery

Because of human cloning and its technology the days of silicone breast implants and other cosmetic procedures that may cause immune disease should soon be over. With the new technology, instead of using materials foreign to the body for such procedures, doctors will be able to manufacture bone, fat, connective tissue, or cartilage that matches the patient's tissues exactly. Anyone will able to have their appearance altered to their satisfaction without the leaking of silicone gel into their

---

With human cloning and its technology it may be possible to ensure that we no longer suffer because of our defective genes

---

bodies or the other problems that occur with present-day plastic surgery. Victims of terrible accidents that deform the face should now be able to have their features repaired with new, safer, technology. Limbs for amputees may be able to be regenerated.

Breast implants

Most people are aware of the breast implant fiasco in which hundreds of thousands of women received silicone breast implants for cosmetic reasons. Many came to believe that the implants were making them ill with diseases of their immune systems. With human cloning and its technology breast augmentation and other forms of cosmetic surgery could be done with implants that would not be any different from the person's normal tissues.

Defective genes

The average person carries 8 defective genes inside them. These defective genes allow people to become sick when they would otherwise remain healthy. With human cloning and its technology it may be possible to ensure that we no longer suffer because of our defe genes.

Down's syndrome

Those women at high risk for Down's syndrome can avoid that risk by cloning.

Tay-Sachs disease

This autosomal recessive genetic disorder could be prevented by using cloning to ensure that a child does not express the gene for the disorder.

Liver failure

We may be able to clone livers for liver transplants.

Kidney failure

We may be able to clone kidneys for kidney transplants.

Leukaemia

We should be able to clone the bone marrow for children and adults suffering from leukaemia. This is expected to be one of the first benefits to come from cloning technology.

Cancer

We may learn how to switch cells on and off through cloning and thus be able to cure cancer. Scientists still do not know exactly how cells differentiate into specific kinds of tissue, nor do they understand why cancerous cells lose their

differentiation. Cloning, at long last, may be the key to understanding differentiation and cancer.

Cystic fibrosis

We may be able to produce effective genetic therapy against cystic fibrosis. Ian Wilmut and colleagues are already working on this problem.

Spinal cord injury

We may learn to grow nerves or the spinal cord back again when they are injured. Quadriplegics might be able to get out of their wheelchairs and walk again. Christopher Reeve, the man who played Superman, might be able to walk again.

Testing for genetic disease

Cloning technology can be used to test for and perhaps cure genetic diseases.

- The above list only scratches the surface of what human cloning technology can do for mankind. The suffering that can be relieved is staggering. This new technology heralds a new era of unparalleled advancement in medicine if people will release their fears and let the benefits begin. Why should another child die from leukaemia when if the technology is allowed we should be able to cure it in a few years' time?

- The above information is an extract from the Human Cloning Foundation's web site which can be found at www.humancloning.org

To clone or not to clone?

Information from CARE (Christian Action Research and Education)

Why use embryos for medical research?

Scientists want to engage in new medical research on embryos because they contain stem cells. These are cells which can develop into any type of body cell, e.g. brain, liver, blood. Scientists believe that research on stem cells removed from embryos will help them understand what makes a stem cell become a blood, bone or heart cell and will lead to new treatment of diseases. They argue that embryonic stem cells will be the best type of cells to investigate.

If an embryo could be produced with the same genetic make-up as a person suffering from a disease and stem cells from that embryo were then able to be grown to new tissues as required, the individual may be cured, because their body would not reject these tissues. Producing compatible tissues/cells is the ultimate aim of the research.

Currently, most 'test tube' embryos are created by the coming together of sperm and eggs, i.e. sexual reproduction. Scientists now want to be able to create embryos by asexual

reproduction to find out if treatments for individuals genetically the same as the embryo would work. They would use a technique known as cell nuclear replacement (CNR) – most often referred to as therapeutic cloning.

CNR involves taking the nucleus of a cell from person A, e.g. a skin cell, which contains A's DNA; taking an egg from person B, with the genetic information from the egg removed, and fusing them together so that the egg from B contains A's DNA. Then an electric current is passed through the 'egg' and it starts dividing as if it had been fertilised. In theory, before this new embryo is 14 days old, stem cells with A's DNA can be removed and treated to develop into new types of cells. The embryo would then be destroyed. These new cells, e.g. blood, pancreas, would then be transplanted to patient A.

Ethical and safety issues

All this sounds good for those who are suffering from incurable and debilitating diseases. So what is the problem?

- creation of embryos for therapeutic cloning crosses a new moral boundary. A person of the same genetic make-up as another is deliberately being created specifically to 'harvest' his or her stem cells before being destroyed – a human being created solely as a means to an end.
- research on stem cells embryos involves the destruction of human life. CARE believes that each embryo is a special person from the moment of conception, and should be treated with dignity.
- in theory an embryo created by CNR could continue to develop into a baby and be born with the same genetic make-up as a person already alive. This is known as reproductive cloning. A number of scientists have acknowledged that allowing therapeutic cloning will inevitably lead to reproductive cloning.

- there are significant safety concerns about using stem cells from embryos created by CNR. Animals created by this method have shown abnormalities.

At the moment, there is almost universal condemnation around the world of human reproductive cloning as ethically unacceptable. The Human Fertilisation and Embryology Authority (HFEA) which licenses all research and treatment in the UK have said they would never license a clinic to produce a full human clone. The Government has stated that they will bring in new legislation at some time in the future to ban reproductive cloning.

Nevertheless, despite a wave of concern, the Government has decided to allow therapeutic cloning – the only government in the European Union to do so – as they see therapeutic and 'reproductive' cloning as entirely separate issues. Parliament has legislated that spare embryos from IVF treatment and embryos created by therapeutic cloning, can be used for stem cell research into medical treatment.

CARE has argued that there is a real alternative to using embryos – one that is completely ethical and has significant potential for treatment. A considerable amount of research shows that stem cells extracted from adults can also be treated so that they can change from one type of cell to another. CARE believes that research funds should be used to investigate further the potential of using adult stem cells, so that using embryos would not be necessary.

- The above information is an extract from the CARE (Christian Action Research and Education) web site which can be found at www.care.org.uk Alternatively, see page 41 for their address details.

© CARE (Christian Action Research and Education)

Who wants to clone?

Information from LIFE

The proponents and opponents of cloning have divided themselves into three distinct groups in the past few years. Below are a few of the most prominent and vocal members of each group, with a few quotes to show their opinions.

Group one: Pro-'full pregnancy' cloning

This group advocates 'full pregnancy' cloning, and wish to help women give birth to copies of other human beings. This group of people would also be in favour of so-called 'therapeutic' cloning, as they would have no ethical objections and would see the technology arising as beneficial to their work.

Severino Antinori and Panayiotis Zavos

Two professors who have many years' experience in IVF and fertility studies. In March 2001 they went public with a plan to begin 'full pregnancy' cloning in an unnamed Mediterranean country, using cloning technology as a method to overcome infertility. Professor Antinori: 'My only aim is to give infertile couples the gift of happiness in the form of children. Cloning is the next step, that's all.'

Randolf H. Wicker

Calling himself 'the world's first human cloning activist', Randolf Wicker runs the web site www.humancloning.org which collects information from around the world. Wicker: 'The most important thing about reproductive human cloning is that it is a reproductive right. That means that every human being has the right to decide if they have children and the manner in which they have them.'

The Raelians

An unusual Canadian cult, formed by an ex-racing driver called Claude Vorihlon who believes that he was abducted and molested by 'voluptuous robots' visiting earth in a UFO in 1973. They believe that mankind was placed on earth by intelligent beings from another planet who produced the first earthmen by cloning techniques. Despite this rather 'interesting' background these people should be taken seriously.

Immediately after Dolly's existence was announced, the Raelians set up a company called Clonaid which advertises on its website that it will 'charge as low as $200,000 US for its cloning services'. Heading up the scientific team is Brigitte Boisselier, a highly qualified French chemist, who is also a Raelian Bishop. Boisselier: 'Our only goal at Clonaid is to develop a safe and reliable way of cloning a human being.' However, despite having little experience in IVF and fertility studies, they do have one major advantage in the race to produce a cloned child: at least 50 young women ready to donate their eggs and carry to term a cloned child. This is usually the bottleneck in the cloning process but by sheer weight of numbers they may be able to overcome it.

Group Two: Anti-'full pregnancy' cloning, but pro-'therapeutic' cloning

This group of people have called for 'full pregnancy' cloning to be outlawed, but are strong proponents of 'therapeutic' cloning, believing that the possible benefits of embryonic stem cells to sufferers of illnesses such as Alzheimer's and Parkinson's far outweigh other ethical considerations.

Donaldson Committee

On 16 August 2000 the Chief Medical Officer, Liam Donaldson, and his committee delivered a long-overdue report entitled *Stem Cell Research: Medical Progress With Responsibility*, which backed 'therapeutic' cloning and advised the Government to legalise it. This committee was set up by the Government and contained a number of eminent scientists, who looked at the evidence for over a year. Lord Donaldson: 'The Committee looked very carefully at the ethical issues and decided the potential benefits outweighed some of the concerns and would be justified by the potential benefits for future generations of patients.'

Tony Blair

In November 2000 Tony Blair gave a speech to the European Bioscience Conference in London, where he told those gathered that the market in Europe alone for biotechnology could be worth over $100 billion and employing three million people by 2005. By coincidence, stem cell technology had been debated in the House of Commons that day, and on this subject he stated that there was 'more than one morally acceptable outcome... Some people are opposed in principle to all forms of embryo research on ethical grounds. But we must also recognise that when stem cell research has huge potential to improve the lives of those suffering from disease, there are also strong ethical arguments in favour so long as clear and effective regulation remains in place.'

Rt Reverend Richard Harries

While some of the leaders of the Church of England have condemned 'therapeutic' cloning, or kept quiet on the subject, Bishop Harries, the Bishop of Oxford, has been one of its loudest proponents. Harries: 'The evidence so far presented – the research that has been printed and the weight of scientific evidence – suggests that research on stem cells derived from embryos is essential.'

Lord Robert Winston

Lord Winston, famous for his BBC television programmes, is also Professor of Fertility at Hammersmith Hospital, London. Despite being a pioneer of IVF and improvements in this field, his views on cloning have been difficult to pin down. However, he certainly voted and argued for the legalisation of 'therapeutic' cloning in the House of Lords in January 2001.

Group Three: Anti-cloning and pro-adult stem cells

This group believe that all cloning is wrong and should be banned, and that we should be concentrating on adult cells, because they will provide the best solution to degenerative disorders.

European Parliament

On 6 September 2000, the European Parliament called for all member states to enact legislation to ban all cloning, 'full pregnancy' and 'therapeutic'. Press Summary: '[The European] Parliament believes that legislators must keep human rights and respect for human dignity and human life constantly in mind. It considers that "therapeutic cloning", which involves the creation of human embryos purely for research purposes, poses an ethical dilemma and crosses a boundary in research norms.' The 1997 European Bioethics Convention would also outlaw 'therapeutic' cloning, as article 18.2 states 'The creation of human embryos for research purposes is prohibited.'

Catholic Church

The Catholic Church has consistently called for all embryo

experimentation to be banned, believing that human life begins at fertilisation and therefore holding that you are killing human life when you carry out such experiments on embryos. This naturally precludes allowing human cloning. The Church's position on embryo research is laid out in documents called *Donum Vitae* and *Evangelium Vitae*.

Other religious leaders

In the run-up to the vote on cloning in the House of Lords in January 2001, an unprecedented coalition of religious leaders asked for an audience with the Prime Minister to express their opposition to cloning. After four requests for a meeting were turned down, they wrote an open letter to every member of the House of Lords. In it they claim that 'the philosophical and ethical implications' of cloning have not been fully considered.

Prolife groups

Prolife groups have been particularly vocal in their condemnation of all forms of cloning. These groups believe that creating human embryos

> *'We have opened the door to yet more deliberate destruction of human life. We are now well on the way towards full reproductive human cloning and it is difficult to see how this can be prevented'*

simply for research purposes is unacceptable, and that human embryos should be accorded the utmost respect. The prolifers also loudly proclaim that 'therapeutic' cloning will inevitably lead to 'full pregnancy', cloning, pointing out that the initial stages in both processes are the same. LIFE: 'We have opened the door to yet more deliberate destruction of human life. We are now well on the way towards full reproductive human cloning and it is difficult to see how this can be prevented.'

Scientists

Some eminent scientists have spoken out against so-called 'therapeutic' human cloning, and one high profile example is Neil Scolding. Professor Scolding is Professor of Clinical Neurosciences at Bristol University. He wrote a letter to the *Lancet* in February 2001, stating that the science used to justify legalising 'therapeutic' cloning is out of date, and we should re-evaluate the potential of adult stem cells. Scolding: 'The past year or two have seen striking advances in our understanding of the biology and potential therapeutic value of stem cells from adult tissue. It is indeed the near breath-taking pace of this research now – four key papers appear in December 2000 alone – that perhaps explains the lack of enthusiasm for embryonic stem cells.'

• The above information is an extract from *Cloning – How it works, who wants to clone and what LIFE thinks. An introduction to Human Cloning* by LIFE Organisation.

© LIFE

17

Reproductive and 'therapeutic' cloning

Information from Comment on Reproductive Ethics (CORE)

What do we mean by human cloning?

Human cloning is the production of a genetic copy of another human organism.

How would we produce human clones?

By (i) embryo splitting – the deliberate division of an early embryo into two or more genetically identical embryos. Embryo splitting can occur naturally (identical multiple births) but remains relatively rare. Surprisingly little is known about natural embryo splitting, suggesting that it should not be used as a model to justify cloning.

or (ii) nuclear transfer – the nucleus of a mature egg cell is removed and replaced with the nucleus of a donor cell from an existing human being. The embryo created by this process will be the clone or twin of the donor of the nucleus.

What is meant by 'reproductive' and 'therapeutic' cloning?

In 'reproductive' cloning the developing embryo (produced by one of the above processes) would be allowed to continue growing as a copy of the donor from whom he or she was created. Reproductive cloning could be used in fertility treatment, to provide a copy of a person we wish to reproduce, or even to provide a living source of 'spare parts' for the donor. Tissue or bone marrow, for example, could be taken from the live clone, or vital organs such as heart or brain harvested.

In 'therapeutic' cloning normal growth of the cloned embryo would not be allowed to continue past the stage (first days of life) when the embryonic cells were not yet fully differentiated. It is thought that these cells (embryonic stem cells) could be programmed to multiply to produce specific human tissue or even organs, which could then be used in transplant therapies. Cell differentiation leading to continued fetal development would not be allowed to take place.

What is the difference between 'reproductive' and 'therapeutic' cloning?

There is absolutely no difference in the initial cloning procedure: a cloned human embryo has to be created in both cases. The difference lies exclusively in the destiny of the clone.

Are there alternatives to 'therapeutic' cloning?

Yes. Cloning may very soon be superseded as a possible avenue for treatment. Exciting new research has discovered stem cells from neural brain stem cells (National Neurological Institute, Milan) and also bone marrow (MCP Hahnemann University, Philadelphia) which seem to have similar properties to the stem cells of the embryo. It is interesting to note that these new possibilities are also more economical

than the proposed cloning procedures, as cloning requires human eggs, which are always in short supply. President Clinton's National Bioethics Advisory Commission suggested that 'because of ethical and moral concerns raised by the use of embryos for research purposes it would be far more desirable to explore the direct use of human cells of adult origin to produce specialised cells or tissue for transplantation into patients.'

Are there any risks associated with cloning?

Many. We need only look at animal studies where very high mortality and abnormality rates are observed. The father of IVF, R.G. Edwards, is one of the many scientists advocating caution in this area. On the subject of cloning, he observes that 'Any clinical applications in human embryology are precluded as long as the reasons for poor success rates, incomplete development and high pre- and perinatal losses in animals …are not fully understood.' (*Human Reproduction Update* Vol.4 No.6 Dec.1998)

Some of the animal abnormalities are 'the consequence of advances driven by biotechnological goals', according to an international team of concerned scientists from York, Louvain and Hamilton (NZ) (*Human Reproduction* Vol.13 Dec.1998). The 'disinterested pursuit of scientific knowledge for its own sake; traditional basic research' (ibid.) is giving way to the commercial drives of the biotechnology industry. Should money influence the moral decision-making process?

Are there other worries associated with human cloning?

There are many social, psychological and moral issues involved. Current concepts of kinship and parenthood become distorted; for example, a boy cloned from his father would be his father's twin brother . . . Creating one human being exclusively for the benefit of another, a utilitarian procedure morally disturbing in itself, may also be psychologically disturbing for the beneficiary . . . Do we wish to create a precedent where the rights of one human being are completely subjugated to the interests or desires of another? . . . Proposals for research on cloned human embryos up to 14 days, followed by compulsory destruction, would have the paradoxical effect of making it a crime *not* to destroy human life . . . Hundreds of thousands of human embryos would be destroyed in such research . . . If the cloned human is of so little value at this early stage, how could we ensure that he or she would be respected if allowed to grow to a later stage of development? . . . Already a clone is perceived as a substandard, second-class human being, otherwise we could not contemplate some of these proposals . . . Would the cloned child who was permitted to survive perceive him or herself as inferior?

How close are we to cloning human beings?

Opinions vary from 18 months to 50 years, with even the suggestion that early human cloning may already have taken place in Korea. Photos circulated recently of an embryo created by Advanced Cell Technology in the United States resulted from an human adult cell nucleus and an enucleated cow's egg. Does this constitute a human embryo? 135 very recent attempts to clone monkeys (Oregon Regional Primate Research Center, Beaverton, Jan. 1999) have resulted in complete failure, which suggests that human cloning is a long way from becoming a reality.

A recommendation . . .

Let us not make decisions in haste.

Even very liberal public bodies world-wide are asking for more time for discussion of these issues. Clinton's National Bioethics Advisory Commission recommends a 3-5-year period of study and reflection 'because of ethical and moral concerns raised by the use of embryos for research'. The European Society of Human Reproduction and Embryology (ESHRE), along with R.G. Edwards, are among others asking for a 5-year moratorium, warning that 'More speculative psychological harms to the child, and effects on the moral, religious and cultural values of society may be enough to justify continued prohibitions in the future, but more time is needed for discussion and evaluation of these concerns.' (ESHRE 1998)

A reflection . . .

If one is opposed to 'reproductive' cloning, can one logically support 'therapeutic' cloning, given that the 'therapeutic' clone is simply a 'reproductive' clone who has not been allowed to continue developing? In this case, to be ethically consistent, one would have to oppose all human cloning.

● The above information is from Comment on Reproductive Ethics (CORE). PO Box 4593, London, SW3 6XE. Tel: 020 7351 1055. Fax: 020 7349 0450. E-mail: info@corethics.org Web site: www.corethics.org

© *Comment on Reproductive Ethics (CORE)*

World ban 'the only way to stop baby cloning'

By Roger Highfield, Science Editor

Nothing short of a worldwide ban on human reproductive cloning will prevent risky and unethical attempts to create duplicate babies, Britain's most eminent academic body said yesterday.

An international moratorium is 'the only way to reduce the chances of such experiments being carried out in other countries', said the Royal Society. But the report to peers said that such a ban must ensure therapeutic cloning research aimed at developing new treatments was not jeopardised.

Earlier this year Prof Severino Antinori, of an infertility unit in Rome, praised 'Tony Blair's intelligent decision' to allow research into therapeutic cloning, the creation of cloned embryos to grow a patient's tissue, and said that it would aid his efforts to create a human clone within two years.

The society's report acknowledged this was the case but said that a ban on therapeutic cloning in Britain would not prevent foreign reproductive cloning but would hamper the development of powerful new treatments.

It was produced at the society's evidence to the House of Lords ad hoc committee on stem cell research.

Stem cells, which hold the key to the ability to grow a patient's own tissue for repair, are central to the cloning debate. Potentially they could be used to create unlimited supplies of replacement tissue, including nerve, bone, skin and heart muscle, for repairing injuries and for treating disease.

Stem cells can be found in adult tissue but the most promising kind, according to many scientists, are found in early human embryos when they consist of only 100 or so cells. Cloning offers a way to grow a patient's own stem cells but, by perfecting such technology, scientists could accelerate efforts to conduct so-called reproductive cloning.

Prof Richard Gardner, who chaired the working group which prepared the report, said: 'When scientists talk about the possible benefits of human reproductive cloning, such as replacing a beloved child or partner lost in an accident, they betray wholly unrealistic expectations about the outcome. While a clone is likely to bear a striking physical resemblance to the original, the two will differ at least as much as identical twins in terms of personality and other higher mental attributes.'

© *Telegraph Group Limited, London 2001*

Are embryonic stem cells a step too far?

Information from the Society, Religion and Technology Project, Church of Scotland

Dolly the cloned sheep has become an icon for biotechnology, with a characteristically post-modern ambivalence. She represents both the hopes and the fears of what embryology and genetics might lead us to. The world's media and many of its leaders set off hares with fears that cloned human beings were just around the corner. In the Church of Scotland, we had already been discussing these issues with the Roslin scientists. We argued that not only would this be ethically unacceptable in principle, it would carry an unacceptably high risk of producing deformed babies. To most people's relief, the fear of human cloning has not materialised. The science has focused on the hopes that Roslin's Dolly technology and other breakthroughs could herald exciting medical benefits. On 19 December 2000, MPs voted to allow research on human embryos as sources of stem cells for treating degenerative diseases. Despite careless use of words, this was not primarily about cloning, but about embryo use.

What are embryonic stem cells?

The present Human Fertilisation and Embryology Act (1990) allows embryo research only for limited purposes mainly to do with infertility. The vote is whether to extend this to allow a potential new use of embryos to make embryonic stem cells. These are special cells in the early embryo before it begins to differentiate. At this point, they can turn into any type of cell in the human body. Two years ago, US scientists found a way to isolate them. Using special chemical treatments, they believe they can direct them into becoming any type of human cell they choose – skin, heart muscle, nerve cells, etc. This opens up a possibility to create

Society, Religion and Technology Project

replacement cells to inject into patients suffering from a wide range of diseases which cause irreversible cell degeneration, like Parkinson's, some heart conditions and diabetes. This is not cloning, but it raises deep ethical concern whether it changes our view and ethical evaluation of the human embryo.

What is the status of the embryo?

There are three positions on this. For two of them, the vote is already quite clear. One extreme sees the early embryo as a ball of cells and nothing more. Because it is undeveloped and would not survive out of the womb, any research is permissible, including the new proposals. The medical benefits, remote as may be, wholly justify the action. At the opposite pole, the Roman Catholic church and many

individual Christians of other denominations, believe that from conception onwards the embryo has the full status of humanity. On principle, this allows no research or use not for the benefit of that particular embryo, including both present and the new potential uses. The Church of Scotland has a middle position, which affirms the special status as created by God, but also recognises potential benefits of embryo research under limited circumstances.

Stepping over a new ethical barrier?

The question for us, and for many who support the current position of the Act, is whether the new applications step over a second ethical barrier. Present research for infertility still treats the embryo as a reproductive entity, for the long-term benefit of other embryos. To use an embryo as a source of body cells is a very different notion both scientifically and ethically. It treats the embryo purely functionally, as a resource and no longer as a whole. The present Act accords the human embryo with a 'special status'. This

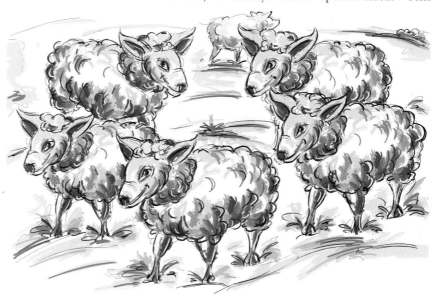

was an ethical compromise, but it restricted the conditions under which embryos can be created or used. The small change now proposed by the Government would push this compromise finally down the 'ball of cells' side. It is hard to see how the embryo would retain any 'special status' if it becomes a routine resource for replacement cells. A 1998 Ministry of Agriculture report into animal cloning cautioned against seeing animals 'merely as means to an end'. Would we now be treating human embryos with less respect than animals?

Are there viable alternatives?

Cell replacement therapy is certainly a goal to pursue, but not at any ethical cost. There have been many statements claiming that there is a complete alternative by deriving stem cells from adults or even umbilical cord blood. We have much sympathy for avoiding embryonic stem cells, but the claims are misleading, and we should be careful not to raise expectations in patients. At present, no one knows. Most of the world's experts on stem cells came to a conference at the Royal Society of Edinburgh in October 2000. Research was reported showing that adult cells are much more adaptable than had been thought. But most considered that embryos' stem cells would still allow treatments for a wider range of diseases than adult cells. Adult cells may carry greater risks; being older they could have developed defects. There is a more radical idea, to adapt Roslin's work to reprogramme ordinary adult non-stem cells directly into the desired type of cell, without intermediate embryos. This is highly speculative, but several methods have been suggested which merit serious research investment. But it would probably mean limited embryo research as a bridge in understanding. For that one purpose personally I might countenance it, on condition that it avoids using embryos routinely.

Where does cloning come into it?

The main source for embryo stem cells would be so-called 'spare'

We now need clear ethical guidelines about what is and what is not a legitimate research proposal. How ironic that we have lines for what may never be done to animals, but not for human embryos

---

embryos left over after IVF treatments, or occasionally embryos created specially for research. Cloning only comes in play if there was a problem of rejection. By definition these cells would be of a different genetic type from the patient. For some diseases cloning might be used to make replacement cells of the same genetic type as the patient, to minimise rejection. A skin or blood sample would be taken from the patient. The Dolly technique would be used to create a temporary cloned embryo, but instead of implanting it to make a cloned baby, it would be used to create genetically matched cells. No one knows yet if it would work, or how often such a route might be preferred over using IVF embryos.

Why we still need a specific vote on embryo cloning

The careless use of the word cloning to describe the whole area of embryonic stem cells has generated much confusion. In fact MPs have not had any chance to vote on the cloning of embryos, because it is technically legal through a loophole in the Act. Ten years ago, Roslin's method of cloning wasn't envisaged and so was not excluded. The Commons vote to allow embryo research into stem cells, also automatically allowed the cloning of embryos, without ever voting on it. The influential European Commission ethical advisory panel reported on these issues last month and drew an ethical line at cloning embryos, as did the European Parliament. Surely it is wrong for the UK Parliament to allow this simply by default. We need early primary

legislation on therapeutic as well as reproductive uses of cloning. The vote should not be seen as a mandate to allow cloned embryos also. That has not been put to a proper democratic test.

Is this the end of special status of the human embryo?

The new regulation is worryingly open ended. Any use of the human embryo for 'increasing knowledge about serious disease' is allowed. On so sensitive a public issue, such indiscriminacy is unwise. In 1990 the HFE Act adopted a strict 'No, unless . . . ' approach. Now we have 'Yes, for everything'. This puts far too much at the discretion of the Human Fertilisation and Embryology Authority. We now need clear ethical guidelines about what is and what is not a legitimate research proposal. How ironic that we have lines for what may never be done to animals, but not for human embryos. It seems we have discarded any remaining notion of Warnock's 'special status' of the human embryo, and reduced it to a mere ball of cells which no one respects.

For further information

The Society, Religion and Technology Project has done extensive work on the ethics of cloning in humans, animals and for medical applications.

SRT Information Sheets

The above information is from an SRT Information Sheet, one in a series aimed at presenting some of the key aspects of current ethical and social issues in technology in simple terms for the non-expert. Other SRT Information Sheets are available on *Patenting, What is Genetic Engineering?, Cloning for Therapeutic Purposes, Human Cloning, Animal Cloning.*

Contact

For more information about this and other ethical issues in technology, contact: Society, Religion and Technology Project , Church of Scotland, John Knox House, 45 High Street, Edinburgh EH1 1SR. Tel : 0131 556 2953, Fax : 0131 556 7478. E-mail: srtp@srtp.org.uk Web site: www.srtp.org.uk

Stem cell therapy

Information from the Medical Research Council (MRC)

What is stem cell therapy?

Stem cell therapy is emerging as a potentially revolutionary new way to treat disease and injury, with wide-ranging medical benefits. It aims to repair damaged and diseased body-parts with healthy new cells provided by stem cell transplants. Bone-marrow transplants used to treat leukaemia patients are a current form of stem cell therapy. The replacement bone-marrow contains blood stem cells which make new, cancer-free, blood cells.

Stem cell therapy research

- Does not necessarily involve cloning.
- Is in its infancy, with much work yet to be done.
- Has potential application in many currently incurable conditions.
- Promising initial results with experimental transplants in humans and animals.
- First clinical applications expected in 5-10 years.
- May one day provide a source of replacement tissues and organs.

The potential benefits of stem cell therapy

Stem cell therapy offers an opportunity to treat many degenerative diseases caused by the premature death or malfunction of specific cell types and the body's failure to replace or restore them. The only hope of complete recovery from such diseases at present is transplant surgery, but there are not enough donors to treat all patients and even when rare donors can be found, this is limited to a few body parts and is very expensive. The best most sufferers of incurable degenerative diseases can expect is treatment to delay the onset, and relieve the symptoms, of ill health caused by their disease.

In theory, stem cells could be collected, grown and stored to provide a plentiful supply of healthy replacement tissue for transplantation into any body site using much less invasive surgery than conven-

tional transplants. Scientists have already reported success with human brain tissue transplants to treat Parkinson's disease and with stem cell-derived mouse heart-muscle cell grafts.

An early stem cell research goal is to find out how to isolate and store stem cells from different tissues. However, adult stem cells are very rare and it is not known whether they are even present in some organs, for example, the heart. Furthermore, they are difficult to extract and grow with currently available techniques.

At first stem cell transplants might be used to encourage the development of new, healthy cells in patients. Later on, when more is understood about how stem cells work, it may be possible to direct stem cells to make healthy replacements for specific cell types that have become damaged or diseased and to use these for transplantation. For example, skin stem cells could generate replacement skin for burns victims. Initially the problem of transplant rejection by the body's immune system that complicates whole organ transplants would also apply to transplants of foreign stem cell material, so stem cell transplants would have to be accompanied by immune system suppressing drugs.

Ideally, scientists would like to discover how to use a patient's own stem cells to create perfectly matched transplant material, or even perhaps to grow replacement organs, avoiding the problems of finding a compatible donor and transplant rejection by the immune system. In the future, this might be achieved by learning how to obtain stem cells from a patient's healthy adult cells.

Stem cell technology will also create new ways to investigate embryonic development, develop new drugs, and test their effects and safety on specific cell types.

What are stem cells?

Stem cells are self-replicating and can also generate a number of more specialised cell types as they multiply. They are plentiful in the early embryo, but scarce and very difficult to find in adult tissues. The variety of other cell types that stem cells can produce becomes severely limited during development.

Totipotent stem cells

At conception, the mother's egg cell and one of the father's sperm cells fuse to create a single cell, called the zygote, which then divides countless times to generate the 216 different cell types that comprise the entire human body.

The zygote and the eight cells created by its first three cell divisions are each capable of developing into a complete human. Such cells are called totipotent. If the dividing cell mass splits apart at this stage, genetically identical embryos are created, as happens in the case of identical twins.

Pluripotent stem cells

As the cells continue to divide, the number of stem cells increases, but the number of different cell types each stem cell can give rise to becomes limited. After five days a hollow ball of cells called the blastocyst forms. The outer blastocyst cell layer forms the placenta, while an inner group of around 50 stem cells is destined to form the developing embryo's tissues. These are pluripotent embryonic stem cells (ES cells). Although they can make most embryonic cell types, they cannot make all the tissues required for complete development.

Multipotent stem cells

Further along the developmental pathway, cells become more and more specialised. Most are eventually committed to a single function, for example to be muscle cells, and lose the ability to do anything else. The process of cellular specialisation is called differentiation and is controlled genetically from the cell's nucleus. The genes necessary for earlier stages of development are programmed to 'switch off' sequentially as differentiation progresses, until only those required for a cell's particular function remain active. A small number of partially differentiated stem cells persist in some adult tissues. These are capable of forming a limited number of specialised cell types and are called multipotent stem cells. Their function is to replace fully differentiated cells that are lost by depletion and damage. For example, bone marrow stem cells replenish different types of blood cell and other kinds of stem cell renew the gut lining.

Which stem cells will be used?

A key goal of stem cell research is to understand how differentiation is controlled and learn how to direct cellular development. Research on both adult and embryonic stem cells will make a complementary contribution to these objectives.

Scientists are investigating how both pluripotent ES cells and different multipotent stem cell types might be used as the basis for developing stem cell therapy. However, many argue that, because of the difficulties of working with adult stem cells, human ES cell research is crucial to the development of stem cell therapies, at least until the programming of cell development is better understood.

Main advantages of pluripotent ES cells:
- Can make many more different cell types than adult stem cells.
- Easier to control growth and differentiation than adult stem cells.
- Relatively much more abundant than adult stem cells and therefore significantly easier to isolate.
- Can use knowledge gained from animal ES cell experiments.

- ES cell research may speed development of adult stem cell therapy techniques.

Human pluripotent stem cells
There are three potential sources of human pluripotent ES cells.
1. Isolation of ES cells from surplus blastocysts created during in-vitro fertilisation (IVF) treatment, which would otherwise be destroyed.
2. Extraction of cells destined to form eggs or sperm from aborted or miscarried fetuses.

Glossary

Stem cell
Multipurpose cells that can make a number of more specialised cell types

Zygote
The single cell formed by the fusion of a stem cell and an egg cell at fertilisation

Totipotent
Cells that can develop into a whole organism

Blastocyst
Ball of around 100 cells formed 5 days after fertilisation

Pluripotent embryonic stem cells (ES cells)
Embryonic stem cells that can make most, but not all, cell types of the developing embryo

Differentiation
The specialisation of cells to perform particular tasks

Nucleus
Contains the genetic material

Multipotent
Adult stem cells that can make limited range of specialised cell types

hPSCs
human pluripotent stem cells

IVF
In-vitro (test tube) fertilisation

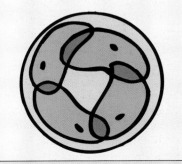

3. Production of tailor-made ES cells from patients' own differentiated adult cells using cloning techniques.

American scientists have used the first two methods to isolate human pluripotent stem cells (hPSCs), and have successfully grown them in the laboratory. Their hPSC cultures can be multiplied indefinitely and are therefore a valuable resource for stem cell research. The work raises the possibility that collections of specific stem cell types could be generated for transplant therapy.

UK research using human embryos is governed by the Human Fertilisation and Embryology Act (1990), which restricts research to embryos no more than 14 days old for certain permitted purposes only. Government widened the Act's scope to include research into stem cell therapies from 31 January 2001, in light of recommendations of the August 2000 Donaldson Report, and following free votes in parliament and in the House of Lords.

The future of stem cell therapy

Scientists think that stem cell therapies could become a clinical reality in 5-10 years' time, but a huge research effort will be needed to achieve this goal.

Stem cell research priorities
- Understanding mechanisms of differentiation and development.
- Identification, isolation and purification of different adult stem cell types.
- Controlling differentiation of stem cells to target cell types needed to treat disease.
- Leaning to make stem cell transplants compatible.
- Demonstrating normal cell development and function and appropriate growth control in stem cell transplants.
- Confirming the results of successful animal experiments in humans.

The MRC already supports fundamental cell and developmental biology research that applies to most of these areas.

© *Medical Research Council (MRC)*

Briefing on non-reproductive cloning

Information from Human Genetics Alert

Introduction

The idea of cloning embryos in order to extract tissues for transplantation is extremely controversial in Britain and around the world. Many people fear that it is a step towards cloned babies and there is widespread feeling that it represents a moral degradation of human life. There are also scientific and legal issues that are currently poorly understood.

Britain is taking an international lead in developing this technology, and this has already attracted concern from other European countries: in September the European Parliament passed a motion censuring the British government for pressing ahead so quickly.[1]

The aim of this article is to clarify some of these issues and to suggest a possible solution: that there should be a moratorium on non-reproductive cloning until there is a global ban on cloning babies and until there has been a chance for a better informed public debate. We argue that a moratorium would not harm progress towards treatments for disease.

Terminology

In this article, we use the term non-reproductive cloning (NRC) to denote the process of (i) creating an embryo by cloning, followed by (ii) extraction of embryonic stem (ES) cells from that embryo, and the use of the ES cells to produce tissues for transplantation. Human Genetics Alert is unhappy with the use of the term 'therapeutic cloning'. Attaching the heavily value-laden word 'therapeutic' tends to silence legitimate concerns about ethical and social issues. The more recent term, 'Cell Nuclear Replacement' adopted by the Donaldson committee[2] is confusing to most people since it attempts to avoid the use of the word cloning, which most people associate with this technology.

Human Genetics Alert

What is non-reproductive cloning?

Cloning is the process of replacing the genetic material of an egg cell with the genetic material of a cell from another embryo, foetus, or an adult. The result is an embryo that is genetically identical to the embryo, foetus or adult from which the new genetic material came.

In NRC, an embryo created in this way would be allowed to grow outside the body until it contained around 100 cells. Amongst these are special cells, known as embryonic stem (ES) cells. In the second stage of the process, these cells would be extracted and grown in tissue culture. The extraction of ES cells would destroy the embryo. The ES cells can be induced to develop into all the different types of cell found in the body, and it is hoped that specialised cells, such as liver cells, could be used for transplantation into patients. If the cell used for creating the initial embryo came from the patient, the liver cells produced would be genetically the same as the patient's and so would not be rejected by the patient's immune system, thus circumventing one of the major problems in transplantation.

An alternative to creating a cloned embryo for each patient would be to use embryos left over from IVF to create banks of ES cells which contained all possible combinations of the proteins that determine whether transplanted tissue matches the patient's immune system. This solution was advocated by the Royal Society as a matter of urgency in its submission to the Donaldson committee.

What are the alternatives?

We should always remember that large reductions in the incidence of disease can be achieved by addressing its environmental and social causes, and this is always preferable to high-tech medical treatments. It is certain that approaches involving NRC will be extremely expensive, and it is

SK

important that they are not allowed to detract or divert resources from the application of preventive medicine or simpler treatments.

A potentially much simpler solution than NRC is to use adult stem cells from the patients themselves. Many organs of the adult body contain stem cells that develop into a narrower range of cell types than ES cells. For example, bone marrow stem cells develop into all the different types of cells found in the blood, but not, normally, nerve or liver cells. Until recently it was believed that such adult stem cells could not change into cells found in another organ. However, in the last two years an increasing number of research papers have been published showing that this is incorrect, and that, for example, neural stem cells can turn into blood cells and muscle cells.

What are the pros and cons of adult and embryonic stem cells?

We should be clear that both of these possibilities are still at a very early stage of development. To date there are only three papers in the scientific literature describing the isolation of human ES cells, even though mouse ES cells have been used for more than 15 years. Human adult stem cells are already being used clinically, but their ability to develop into cells from other organs is a new discovery. Unfortunately, there has been a huge amount of hype surrounding the idea of NRC and many patients, such as those suffering from Parkinson's disease, have been led to believe that they may personally benefit from treatments based on ES cells. It is unlikely that this will happen, since there is at least ten years of fundamental research and development needed before such techniques are clinically applied.

Many scientists are excited by the potential of NRC to tackle medical problems for which we currently have no good solution. However, ES cells have a number of drawbacks which have not been sufficiently acknowledged. The first of these is that we do not know how to control the way that ES cells develop into different cell types. It is not certain that we will ever be able

---

There should be a moratorium on non-reproductive cloning until there is a global ban on cloning babies and until there has been a chance for a better informed public debate

---

to do this reliably, and it will be extremely technically difficult to produce 100% pure populations of a particular type of cell. It has also been suggested that we will be able to produce whole organs for transplantation, but this presents an even greater challenge, because organs contain different types of cells in a complex architecture. A further problem with ES cells is their tendency to form tumours when transplanted; that is why it would be essential to produce 100% pure cultures of specialised cells. Other problems with ES cells produced by cloning is that the cloning process may lead to abnormal cell behaviour. Many of the animals produced by cloning have been abnormal or have died very shortly after birth. These problems mean that cells derived from ES cells would have to be very extensively tested before they could be used for transplantation.

It is clear that adult stem cells are not as versatile as ES cells. However, this may be an advantage, since they may be easier to control. Adult stem cells are not currently available in large quantities and grow slowly, so it is not certain that it will be possible to create sufficient tissue for transplantation.

In summary, both stem cell approaches have potential and both face major challenges. The NRC approach is extremely ambitious and involves many entirely new techniques. It is by no means certain that it will ever be made to work. We are very concerned by the recent report of the Royal Society[3] which attempted to talk down adult stem cells whilst glossing over the problems with NRC.

How is the moral status of embryos affected by non-reproductive cloning?

Human Genetics Alert is not a 'pro-life' organisation, and we do not believe that embryos have the same moral status as human beings. It is unfortunate that because the debate in the media on this issue has been dominated by pro-life organisations and scientists, the impression has been given that it is only those who believe that the embryo is a person who have ethical concerns about cloning and then destroying embryos. We believe that the majority of the public occupies a middle ground between the two polarised extremes, but unfortunately their views have barely been heard.

In fact, current UK law is based on the concept that embryos must be treated with respect, even though they are not regarded as persons. We would argue that the creation of embryos purely as a source of biological material degrades their moral status, since it makes them nothing more than means to achieving the desired end. It would seem ridiculous to speak of respect for something that has been created simply in order to extract certain useful cells: it becomes a mere thing. The US Patent and Trademark Office has already stated that it would grant patents on human embryos, and this year has seen the revelation that several companies, as well as the leading ES cells researcher in this country, have sought patents on human embryos. This concern about instrumentalising embryos is the reason why all European countries with the exception of the UK prohibit the creation of embryos solely for purposes of research. Even in Britain, this has been done extremely rarely, but it would massively increase if NRC were to be widely used.

It should be noted that the use of surplus embryos for research does not degrade embryos' moral status in the same way. In this case their essential function and moral meaning as potential human beings, which is defined by the purpose for which they were created, is not affected.

Another way of understanding this concern is that NRC turns

reproduction, with all its social and human significance, into just another production process. The production of tissues for transplantation through NRC, although it would produce individually customised products, is nonetheless a production process which would operate on an industrial scale.

Whilst the Donaldson committee recognised these concerns, it did not adequately address them. Instead it simply adopted the utilitarian argument that humans would benefit medically from the reduction of embryos' moral status. Whilst medical benefit is a relevant moral consideration, it is not the only one. We believe that the tendency to turn human life into a mere thing is part of a broader tendency promoted by reproductive and genetic technologies. The implications of such a trend for our concepts of human dignity and human rights need to be taken extremely seriously. This does not mean that NRC is automatically ethically unacceptable, but this issue clearly deserves more public debate than it has received to date. We believe that it is vital that there be such a public debate before NRC is allowed to proceed.

References
1 European Parliament Resolution B5-710, 751, 753 and 764/2000 adopted 7th September 2000.
2 *Stem Cell Research: Medical Progress with Responsibility* Department of Health August 2000.
3 *Stem cell research and therapeutic cloning: an update* Royal Society document 12/00, November 2000.

• Copies of this article can be obtained from Human Genetics Alert, PO Box 6313, London N16 0DY Phone: 020 8809 4513. Or see their web site at www.hgalert.org

International moratorium on human cloning

International moratorium on human cloning should be considered

An international moratorium on human reproductive cloning should be considered by policy-makers because it is the only way to reduce the chances of such experiments being carried out in other countries, according to a Royal Society report published today (20 June 2001). But a moratorium must include provisions to ensure that research on stem cells and therapeutic cloning is not jeopardised.

Research into therapeutic cloning in the UK, which would be permitted by the changes to the 1990 Human Fertilisation and Embryology Act, may lead to a significant increase in the likelihood that human reproductive cloning will be successfully carried out in other countries where it is not outlawed, the Society acknowledges in its evidence to the House of Lords Ad Hoc Committee on Stem Cell Research.

The Society points out that a ban on therapeutic cloning in the UK would not prevent research on reproductive cloning in other countries, but would hamper the development of powerful new therapies for degenerative diseases.

The Society pledges its support for legislation to outlaw human reproductive cloning in the UK.

Professor Richard Gardner, who chaired the working group that prepared the Society's evidence, said: 'We think that a ban on reproductive cloning would have public support and is currently justified on scientific grounds. It would also help to improve the public's confidence in science.'

The report highlights the hazards of experiments on human reproductive cloning. Prof Gardner

said: 'Our experience with animals suggests that there would be a very real danger of creating seriously handicapped individuals if anybody tries to implant cloned human embryos into the womb.'

Professor Gardner said: 'There has been a lot of unchallenged publicity this year for groups who claim that they will clone human beings in the next few years. It is the Royal Society's view that this would be unethical and that responsible scientists across the world should not ignore the public's well-founded opposition to such research.'

Prof Gardner added: 'When these scientists talk about the possible benefits of human reproductive cloning, such as replacing a beloved child or partner lost in an accident, they betray wholly unrealistic expectations about the outcome. While a clone is likely to bear a striking physical resemblance to the original, the two will differ at least as much as identical twins in terms of personality and other higher mental attributes.'

The Society also reiterates its belief that there should be no delay to see whether either adult or embryonic stem cells will provide all of the urgently needed therapies, and that research on both types of stem cells should be pursued in parallel.

Prof Gardner said: 'Adult stem cells are small in number and often hard to access. We have to acknowledge that, with very few exceptions like bone marrow, adult stem cells will be only obtainable from organs of people shortly after death. Since there is already an acute shortage of donors of organs for transplantation, work on adult stem cells is going to entail even greater competition for scarce resources.'

Notes

1. The Royal Society is an independent academy promoting the natural and applied sciences. Founded in 1660, the Society has three roles, as the UK academy of science, as a learned Society, and as a funding agency. It responds to individual demand with selection by merit, not by field. The Society's objectives are to:
- recognise excellence in science
- support leading-edge scientific research and its applications
- stimulate international inter-action
- further the role of science, engineering and technology in society
- promote education and the public's understanding of science
- provide independent authorita-tive advice on matters relating to science, engineering and technology
- encourage research into the history of science

© The Royal Society

Scientists boycott 'human clone' conference

Fertility experts and leading scientists are to boycott a forthcoming conference on cloning that will be presided over by Dr Severino Antinori, the doctor who plans to clone the first human baby.

A member of Britain's IVF watchdog and the scientist who cloned Dolly the sheep had been criticised because they planned to speak at the 'First International Symposium on Cloning' because of its president's highly-publicised plan to create the first human clone. The symposium is being held in Monte Carlo next month.

Dr Anne McLaren, a member of the Human Fertilisation and Embryology Authority, and Prof Ian Wilmut of the Roslin Institute, Edinburgh, where Dolly was cloned, had originally agreed to attend because it was the Third World Congress (TWC) of A Part (Association of Private Assisted Reproductive Technology Clinics and Laboratories).

Yesterday, however, it emerged that the managing board of A Part has voted to cut ties with the Monte Carlo conference and now plans its own congress next year. Dr McLaren said that she would now pull out and the Roslin confirmed that Prof Wilmut would also do so.

'My motivation was to make sure that other private IVF practitioners knew what they would be getting into. There is no point in trying to

By Roger Highfield, Science Editor

warn Antinori,' she said. Dr Antinori said the meeting would go ahead and added: 'The votes must be considered not effective since some of the 12 members have . . . resigned.'

Prof Wilfried Feichtinger, President of A Part, said in an email and message on the A Part web site: 'Dr Antinori's appearances and commentary over the past months have attracted much unfavourable attention.

Plans by Dr Antinori of the Rome-based Raprui clinic to create the first human clone have been vehemently opposed by the vast majority of scientists

'Italian friends of mine, not connected with A Part, have communicated this to me, as have some of you. His coverage in the European and American media reflects badly on him and has at least the potential to reflect badly on A Part.

'Over the past few months, and increasingly in the last two weeks, A Part members and managing board members have expressed serious concerns about the TWC to me. As president of A Part, I became gravely concerned. In March of this year, Dr Antinori said that he would personally assume complete financial responsibility for the congress.

'Later, I learned that Dr Antinori had also taken over all decision making, refusing to involve his co-organisers. Since then the A Part secretariat has not been given any information about the finances and the planning of this meeting,' said Prof Feichtinger.

The managing board of A Part, which includes Dr Antinori, voted overwhelmingly to postpone the congress after becoming concerned by a number of problems: no abstracts had been submitted to the journal that would accompany the meeting; 41 of the 77 speakers have so far not signed up; registrations are poor and of 46 guests, 19 have announced their withdrawal within the past few weeks.

Plans by Dr Antinori of the Rome-based Raprui clinic to create the first human clone have been vehemently opposed by the vast majority of scientists. They have pointed out the inefficiency of cloning and the likelihood of its high mortality rate.

© Telegraph Group Limited, London 2001

Cloning – the fountain of youth and never-ending drugs

In 1999, a study on Dolly, the world's first cloned sheep, showed that her cells appeared prematurely old. Scientists had previously speculated that Dolly might have a shortened life span because the cells used to clone her came from a comparatively old animal in ovine terms.

In April, researchers from the Advanced Cell Technology (ACT), Massachusetts claimed that they had cloned six heifers – Lily, Daffodil, Crocus, Forsythia, Rose and Persephone – which were showing signs of being even younger than their actual ages, suggesting that cloning technology offered a 'fountain of youth'.

In announcing the discovery, Dr Robert Lanza of ACT said that the results show that cloning actually has the potential to reverse the ageing of cells and has 'profound implications for treating age-related disease and for understanding the actual mechanisms behind the ageing process'.[1]

In January 2001, scientists from ACT announced that the first cloned animal from an endangered species had been born. The animal, a gaur, is a wild ox and the breed is native to India, Indo-China and Southeast Asia. The species has been hunted for sport for generations and is also threatened by the destruction of its forest habitats.

The scientists had taken a skin cell from a dead male gaur and fused it with an egg cell from a domestic cow from which the DNA had been removed. ACT believed the technology would enable it to eradicate the threat of extinction for endangered species.

However, hopes that endangered species could survive with the help of cloning techniques that used surrogate mothers from related species were dashed when the baby gaur, named Noah, died of a bacterial intestinal infection 48

Advocates for Animals

hours after his birth. Undeterred, ACT is now considering cloning giant pandas using black bears as surrogates and has even turned its attention to the recently extinct Pyrenees bucardo goat. The Spanish Government has already given ACT its approval to produce clones of the bucardo using normal goats to carry the embryos.[2]

Meanwhile, in December, MPs voted to allow scientists to clone human embryos up to 14 days old and extract from them stem cells, the unprogrammed cells with the potential to become any type of human tissue. One month later, the House of Lords added its support to extend the law on embryo research.[3]

Days before the House of Lords' vote, the Raelian Movement, a world-wide cult whose members believe that the human race was cloned by aliens, claims to have received £350,000 from an American couple to clone their dead 10-month-

old daughter. The couple has already given skin cells from their daughter to scientists who say they can produce her clone by the end of 2001. The cult claims to have up to 50 surrogate mothers who have already volunteered to carry cloned human embryos. The announcement adds to fears of a future of uncontrolled cloning laboratories operating in America. Human cloning is not yet banned in the United States.[4]

The fears were heightened when an Italian fertility expert, Dr Severino Antinori, said he would 'attempt to clone a human within the next year and had ten couples who were potential candidates for the procedure'.[5]

References
1. *New Scientist*, 6 May 2000.
2. *Nature*, Vol 409, 277, London – 18 January 2001.
3. *The Daily Telegraph*, London – 15 January 2001.
4. Ibid – 3 January 2001.
5. *Evening News*, Edinburgh – 27 January 2001.

• The above information is an extract from the *Eighty-ninth Annual report* of Advocates for Animals. See page 41 for their address details.

FOUNTAIN OF YOUTH

Animal cloning

Information from the Research Defence Society (RDS)

Dolly the sheep may be the world's most famous clone, but she is not the first. Cloning creates a genetically identical copy of an animal or plant. Many animals – including frogs, mice, sheep, and cows – had been cloned before Dolly. Plants are often cloned – when you take a cutting, you are producing a clone. Human identical twins are also clones.

So Dolly is not the first clone, and she looks like any other sheep, so why did she cause so much excitement and concern? Because she was the first mammal to be cloned from an adult cell, rather than an embryo. This was a major scientific achievement, but also raised ethical concerns. Since Dolly was born in 1996, other sheep have been cloned from adult cells, as have mice, pigs, goats and cattle.

How was Dolly produced?

Producing an animal clone from an adult cell is obviously much more complex and difficult than growing a plant from a cutting. So when scientists working at the Roslin Institute in Scotland produced Dolly, the only lamb born from 277 attempts, it was a major news story around the world.

To produce Dolly, the scientists used the nucleus of an udder cell from a six-year-old Finn Dorset white sheep. The nucleus contains nearly all the cell's genes. They had to find a way to 'reprogramme' the udder cells – to keep them alive but stop them growing – which they achieved by altering the growth medium. Then they injected the cell into an unfertilised egg cell which had had its nucleus removed, and made the cells fuse by using electrical pulses. The unfertilised egg cell came from a Scottish Blackface ewe.

When the scientists had managed to fuse the nucleus from the adult white sheep cell with the egg cell from the black-faced sheep, they needed to make sure that the resulting cell would develop into an embryo. They cultured it for six or seven days to see if it divided and developed normally, before implanting it into a surrogate mother, another Scottish Blackface ewe.

From 277 cell fusions, 29 early embryos developed and were implanted into 13 surrogate mothers.

But only one pregnancy went to full term, and the 6.6kg Finn Dorset lamb 6LLS (alias Dolly) was born after 148 days.

Why are scientists interested in cloning?

The main reason that the scientists at Roslin wanted to be able to clone sheep and other large animals was connected with their research aimed at producing medicines in the milk of such animals. Researchers have managed to transfer human genes that produce useful proteins into sheep and cows, so that they produce, for instance, the blood clotting agent factor IX to treat haemophilia or alpha-1-antitrypsin to treat cystic fibrosis and other lung conditions. But the techniques used in this gene transfer are a bit hit and miss. Finding

Attitudes towards life sciences

Results from a poll by the MORI Social Research Institute on behalf of Novartis about attitudes toward the life sciences were released at the BAAS (British Association for the Advancement of Science) Annual Conference in 1999.

Q. Which, if any, of the following do you support and which do you oppose?	Support	Oppose	Don't know
Scientific experiments on live animals	31%	60%	8%
Cloning of animals such as Dolly the sheep	16%	74%	9%
Cloning and growing of human cells	28%	60%	11%
Genetic modification of plants	20%	62%	16%
Genetic modification of animals	16%	71%	11%
Human genetic testing for diseases	66%	20%	11%
Transplants of organs into humans from human donors	90%	6%	3 %
Transplants of organs into humans from animal donors	44%	42%	13%

Source: MORI (Market & Opinion Research International Limited)

a more precise way of inserting these genes into an adult cell and then using the cell to produce a cloned animal would be a much better way to produce founder animals which would then breed conventionally to form flocks of genetically engineered animals all producing medicines in their milk.

There are other medical and scientific reasons for the interest in cloning. It is already being used alongside genetic techniques in the development of animal organs for transplant into humans (xeno-transplantation). Combining such genetic techniques with cloning of pigs (achieved for the first time in March 2000) would lead to a reliable supply of suitable donor organs.

The study of animal clones and cloned cells could lead to greater understanding of the development of the embryo and of ageing. Cloning could be used to create better animal models of diseases, which could in turn lead to further progress in understanding and treating those diseases. It could even enhance biodiversity by ensuring the continuation of rare breeds and endangered species.

What has happened to Dolly?

Dolly, probably the most famous sheep in the world, lives a pampered existence at the Roslin Institute. She has mated and produced normal offspring in the normal way, showing that such cloned animals can reproduce. Her chromosomes are a little shorter than those of other sheep, but in other ways she's the same as any other sheep of her chronological age. Study of her cells has also revealed that the very small amount of DNA outside the nucleus, in the mitochondria of the cells, is all inherited from the donor egg cell, not from the donor nucleus like the rest of her DNA. So she is not a completely identical copy. This finding could be important for diseases like certain neuromuscular, brain and kidney conditions that are passed on through the mother's side of the family only.

Ethical concerns and regulation

Most of the ethical concerns about cloning relate to the possibility that it might be used to clone humans. There would be enormous technical difficulties. As the technology stands at present, it would have to involve women willing to donate perhaps hundreds of eggs, surrogate pregnancies with high rates of miscarriage and stillbirth, and the possibility of premature ageing and high cancer rates for any children so produced.

In the USA, President Clinton asked the National Bioethics Commission and Congress to examine the issues, and in the UK the House of Commons Science and Technology Committee, the Human Embryology and Fertilisation Authority and the Human Genetics Advisory Commission all consulted widely and advised that human cloning should be banned. The Council of Europe has banned human cloning: in fact most countries have banned the use of cloning to produce human babies (human reproductive cloning). However, there is one important medical aspect of cloning technology that could be applied to humans, which people may object to less. This is therapeutic cloning (or cell nucleus replacement) for tissue engineering, in which tissues, rather than a baby, are created.

In therapeutic cloning, single cells would be taken from a person and 'reprogrammed' to create stem cells, which have the potential to develop into any type of cell in the body. When needed, the stem cells could be thawed and then persuaded to grow into particular types of cell such as heart or brain cells that could be used in medical treatment.

Therapeutic cloning research is already being conducted in animals, and stem cells have been grown by this method and transplanted back into the original donor animal. In humans, this technique would revolutionise cell and tissue transplantation as a method of treating diseases. However, it is a very new science and has raised ethical concerns. In the UK a group headed by the Chief Medical Officer, Professor Liam Donaldson, has recommended that research on early human embryos should be allowed. This will require a change in the law and has yet to be debated in parliament.

As far as animal cloning is concerned, all cloning for research or medical purposes in the UK must be approved by the Home Office under the strict controls of the Animals (Scientific Procedures) Act 1986. This safeguards animal welfare while allowing important scientific and medical research to go ahead.

Further information

The Roslin Institute has lots of information about the research that led to Dolly, and the scientific studies of Dolly, as well as links to many other sites that provide useful information on the scientific and ethical aspects of this research.

PPL Therapeutics plc has used the nuclear transfer cloning technique licensed from the Roslin Institute to create cloned sheep with genetic modifications and cloned pigs.

The report of the Chief Medical Officer's Expert Advisory Group on Therapeutic Cloning: *Stem cell research: medical progress with responsibility* is available from the UK Department of Health, PO Box 777, London SE1 6XH.

Further information on therapeutic cloning and stem cell research is available from the Medical Research Council.

Interesting illustrated features on cloning have been published by *Time, Scientific American,* and *New Scientist.* BBC News Online has a Q&A *What is Cloning?*

Ethical aspects of animal cloning

A view from the Dr Hadwen Trust for Humane Research

Ethical aspects of animal cloning

Cloning and the genetic modification of animals (which are closely allied technologies) breach the intrinsic value of individual animals and of distinct animal species. It treats sentient animals – capable of experiencing pain, distress, suffering and lasting harm[1] – as though they have only instrumental value.

There are several different methods of cloning, and in the last five years cows, goats, mice, pigs and sheep have been cloned. Apart from cloning 'just to see if it can be done', cloning research aims to develop animals as convenient production units:

- as inexpensive 'bioreactors' to produce proteins in their milk or urine;
- as living factories with genetically modified spare parts for transplantation into humans (xeno-transplantation);
- as high-profit meat-, or milk-producing animals.

All of these negate the individuality and ignore the sentience of these animals.

Suffering and lives wasted

Cloning is wasteful in animal suffering and animal lives, because of its gross inefficiency. Dolly the cloned sheep was the only survivor out of 277 cloned embryos. Typically, out of 100 attempts to clone an animal only one or two live offspring result.[2,3] When an embryo does implant successfully in the womb of the surrogate mother, pregnancies often end in miscarriage which can cause pain and distress.

Moreover, a significant number of births are difficult, especially because many embryos grow to an unusually large size (large offspring syndrome); a proportion of the offspring die shortly after birth; and some of those who survive have 'serious developmental ab-normalities'.[2] These include under-developed lungs, severe bloodstream imbalances, abnormalities of the kidneys, liver and brain, enlarged tongues, intestinal blockages, diabetes, immune deficiencies and shortened tendons.[4]

A paper published in 1999 described the pathological features of cloned transgenic calves.[5] The placenta of one calf was six times the normal size, and after birth its bloodstream oxygen and carbon dioxide levels were severely abnormal; it died after one day. Autopsy revealed an enlarged heat and malformed liver as well as under-developed lungs. The cow herself suffered a fatal drop in blood pressure after giving birth; in this particular study four out of 12 surrogate cows died from complications of pregnancy.

Legislation and public concern

In Britain animal experimentation is governed by the Animals (Scientific Procedures) Act. A

pivotal feature of the Act is that the Home Secretary must perform a cost/benefit assessment before permitting a programme of animal experiments. The costs are borne by the animals used, in terms of pain, distress and loss of life. The benefits tend mainly to accrue to humans.

Because cloning has such a high failure rate and is so wasteful of animals' lives, and because any potential benefit is so speculative, we question whether the cost/benefit assessment is being, or even can be, carried out in a proper manner. If it is not, then the licensing of much cloning research may actually be in breach of the law.

Finally, numerous opinion polls, including the EU-wide Eurobaro-meter survey, show that the public is concerned about the ethical, animal welfare and safety issues in biotechnology. We believe that the law, as it is being applied, does not reflect this genuine public concern.

References
1 As described in British legislation, the Animals (Scientific Procedures) Act 1986.
2 *Science*, 2000, vol. 288 p. 722.
3 *Nature*, 2000, vol. 407, pp. 86-90.
4 *New Scientist*, 2001, 19 May pp. 14-15.
5 *Theriogenology*, 1999, vol. 51, p. 1452.

• The Dr Hadwen Trust for Humane Research is a registered medical research charity. We were founded on anti-vivisection principles and are opposed in principle to all animal experiments, for both ethical and scientific reasons. The Trust's aims are to encourage, fund and promote the development and use of non-animal methods to replace animal experiments in medical research. See their web site at www.drhadwentrust.org.uk or page 41 for their address details.

Cloning

Information from BUAV

Introduction

Cloning is the production of genetically identical animals using laboratory grown cells. Until this decade all animals multiplied by egg fertilisation via sexual reproduction. In 1995, scientists at the Roslin Institute in Scotland produced Megan and Morag: two Welsh lambs cloned from a single embryo, they were the first cloned mammals in the world. In 1997, Dolly hit the headlines; unlike Megan and Morag, she was a clone produced not from an embryonic cell but from the mammary gland cells of a mature six-year-old ewe. This work has shattered the belief of many biologists that cells from adult mammals cannot be persuaded to regenerate a whole animal.

Animal welfare problems

From the diagram it can be seen that the clone is a result of four separate surgical operations on the donor and recipient ewes. The cloned Dolly embryo was surgically implanted into a temporary recipient ewe who was killed six days later. The cloned embryo was then examined, deemed viable and implanted into another ewe. These operations are highly invasive and can be very stressful to the animal involved. Significant manipulation of the ovulation and oestrus cycle of the sheep is also needed which includes exposing the animals to a wide range of hormones. The collection of eggs, implantation of embryos and exposure to additional hormones can all exert an intolerable level of stress on the animal, severely undermining its general welfare.

The cloning technique described is still a very imprecise technology. To produce Megan and Morag, 250 embryos were produced. Of these only 34 could be used. Five produced lambs but three of these lambs died immediately after birth because their internal organs were malformed. One of the surrogate mother ewes had to deliver by caesarean section primarily because the lamb she was carrying was so huge.[1] The lamb weighed 15lb whereas the average weight of the Welsh Mountain lamb is about 8lb, a fact that the Roslin team entirely omitted from their original paper. When the story was leaked to the press they had to take the unusual step of printing a letter in the journal *Nature* detailing the effects.[2]

With Dolly, out of 277 cell fusions only 29 cells began growing in culture. All 29 were implanted into receptive ewes but only a single cloned lamb was produced.[3] This is a success rate of only 0.36%. Whereas, in nature between 33-50% of all fertilised eggs develop into newborns.

As Dolly is cloned from a six-year-old sheep (old in sheep terms), it is unknown whether she will have a shortened life span. There is also an increased chance of Dolly developing cancer, as the cell's DNA blueprint (being so old) may have been damaged.

More problems

Cloning omits the need for sexual reproduction but it is through this means that different gene combinations are created that give new beneficial characteristics to species, such as resistance to disease. In fact many farmers are not interested in producing clones of 'their prize milk producing cow' purely because of the danger that the whole herd would be susceptible and die from the same disease (or other disasters). Old-fashioned selective breeding methods are still more efficient ways of producing large numbers of genetically altered animals. But even this well-known technique has produced animals with a wealth of animal welfare problems. Rapid growth in broiler chickens has caused crippling deformities of limb bones and joints[4] and turkeys have been bred with such large chest muscles that they can no longer mate naturally.[5]

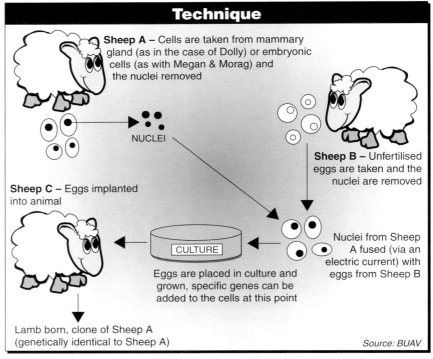

Technique

Sheep A – Cells are taken from mammary gland (as in the case of Dolly) or embryonic cells (as with Megan & Morag) and the nuclei removed

NUCLEI

Sheep B – Unfertilised eggs are taken and the nuclei are removed

Sheep C – Eggs implanted into animal

CULTURE

Nuclei from Sheep A fused (via an electric current) with eggs from Sheep B

Eggs are placed in culture and grown, specific genes can be added to the cells at this point

Lamb born, clone of Sheep A (genetically identical to Sheep A)

Source: BUAV

There are serious concerns that the technique used to create Dolly may not even work in other species. It has been suggested that sheep embryos only utilise the DNA in the nucleus after 3-4 cell divisions, which will give the egg cell sufficient time to reprogramme the DNA from the mammary cell functions to egg cell functions.[6] All attempts to clone mice from adult mouse cells have failed. Mice and human cells use the nuclear DNA much earlier than sheep and may not be capable of cloning.

Purpose of cloning

The main purpose of cloning is to find a more effective way of mass producing genetically engineered animals that will make them more desirable for agriculture or medicine. Cloned animals will be living factories that will be able to produce a range of human drugs. Livestock could be mass produced to be of specific dimensions to satisfy the meat industry.

Cloning mammals means that you can use larger animals for types of studies that were previously reserved for genetically engineered mice. In the past it was not practical to use larger mammals because of a combination of the inefficiency of the technology and the long periods of gestation of the offspring. Now technically you could take an egg of any mammal, insert a gene for a particular human disease and clone it to produce an entire herd with that particular disease, or any other scientifically desired feature. Animal breeding companies, race horsing stables and kennel club owners are already showing an interest in the use of this technology to multiply their best animals.

PPL Therapeutics, a UK based biotechnology company who have the rights to use the Roslin cloning technique, are looking into creating genetically engineered animals that would have organs suitable for human transplants. Once they have created such an animal they could mass produce it via the cloning technique.

Another possible use of cloning could be to save endangered species. Cells could be taken from rare creatures, embryos created and implanted into surrogate mothers. However, cloning will decrease the genetic diversity of the species. If a cloned animal was susceptible to a disease or developed a disease then the rest of the clones would also fall victim. However, cloning is not the answer to save animals threatened with extinction. In fact the main threats to endangered species are from loss of habitat, pollution.

References
1 Miller, A., (16/03/96), Have we, with sheep, gone astray, *The Tablet*.
2 Campbell, K.H.S., McWhir, J., Ritchie, W.A. and Wilmut, I. (1996), Implications of cloning, *Nature*, Vol. 380, Correspondence, p. 383.
3 Viable offspring derived from fetal and adult mammalian cells. (1997), *Nature*, Vol. 385, p. 810.
4 Webster, J. (1990), Animal welfare and genetic engineering, in: *The bio-revolution, cornucopia or Pandora's box*. Eds. Wheale, P. and McNally, R.
5 D'Silva, J. and Stevenson, P. (1995), *Modern breeding technologies of farm animals*. A Compassion in World Farming Trust, Ed. O'Brien, T.
6 Bohlin, R. (1997), The little lamb that made a monkey of us all. Can humans be cloned like sheep? www.leadru.com/orgs/probe

Cloning animals

Information from the Roslin Institute

Much confusion happens when people see the word 'clone' used. Depending on the age of the dictionary, the definition of biological cloning can be:

- A group of genetically identical individuals descended from the same parent by asexual reproduction. Many plants show this by producing suckers, tubers or bulbs to colonise the area around the parent.
- A group of genetically identical cells produced by mitotic division from an original cell. This is where the cell creates a new set of chromosomes and splits into two daughter cells. This is how replacement cells are produced in your body when the old ones wear out.
- A group of DNA molecules produced from an original length of DNA sequences produced by a bacterium or a virus using molecular biology techniques. This is what is often called molecular cloning or DNA cloning.
- The production of genetically identical animals by 'embryo splitting'. This can occur naturally at the two cell stage to give identical twins. In cattle, when individual cells are taken from 4- and 8-cell embryos and implanted in different foster mothers, they can develop normally into calves and this technique has been used routinely within cattle breeding schemes for over 10 years.
- The creation of one or more genetically identical animals by transferring the nucleus of a body cell into an egg from which the nucleus has been removed. This is also known as Nuclear Transfer (NT) or cell nuclear replacement (CNR) and is how Dolly was produced.

Technology

Nuclear transfer involves transferring the nucleus from a diploid cell (containing 30-40,000 genes and a full set of paired chromosomes) to an unfertilised egg cell from which the maternal nucleus has been removed. The technique involves several steps. The nucleus itself can be transferred or the intact cell can be injected into the oocyte. In the latter case, the oocyte and donor cell are normally fused and the 'reconstructed embryo' activated by a short electrical pulse. In sheep, the embryos are then cultured for 5-6 days and those that appear to be developing normally (usually about 10%) are implanted into foster mothers.

Nuclear transfer is not a new technique. It was first used in 1952 to study early development in frogs and in the 1980s the technique was used to clone cattle and sheep using cells taken directly from early embryos. In 1995, Ian Wilmut, Keith Campbell and colleagues created live lambs – Megan and Morag – from embryo derived cells that had been cultured in the laboratory for several weeks. This was the first time live animals had been derived from cultured cells and their success opened up the possibility of introducing much more precise genetic modifications into farm animals.

In 1996, Roslin Institute and collaborators PPL Therapeutics created Dolly, the first animal cloned from a cell taken from an adult animal. The announcement of her birth in February 1997 started the current fascination in all things cloned. Until then, almost all biologists thought that the cells in our bodies were fixed in their roles: the creation of Dolly from a mammary gland cell of a six-year-old sheep showed this was not the case and the achievement was voted Science Breakthrough of the Year at the end of 1997.

Progress AD (After Dolly)

At first Dolly was a 'clone alone' but in August 1998, a group in Hawaii published a report of the cloning of over 50 mice by nuclear transfer. Since then, research groups around the world have reported the cloning of cattle, sheep, mice, goats and pigs. Equally competent groups have had no success in cloning rabbits, rats, monkeys, cats or dogs.

There are differences in early development between species that might influence success rate. In sheep and humans, the embryo divides to between the 8- and 16-cell stage before nuclear genes take control of development, but in mice this transition occurs at the 2-cell stage. In 1998, a Korean group claimed that they had cloned a human embryo by nuclear transfer but their experiment was terminated at the 4-cell stage and so they had no evidence of successful reprogramming.

Success rates remain low in all species, with published data showing on average only about 1% of 'reconstructed embryos' leading to live births. With unsuccessful attempts at cloning unlikely to be published, the actual success rate will be substantially lower. Many cloned offspring die late in pregnancy or soon after birth, often through respiratory or cardiovascular dysfunction. Abnormal development of the placenta is common and this is probably the major cause of foetal loss earlier in pregnancy. Many of the cloned cattle and sheep that are born are much larger than normal and apparently normal clones may have some unrecognised abnormalities.

The high incidence of abnormalities is not surprising. Normal development of an embryo is dependent on the methylation state of the DNA contributed by the sperm and egg and on the appropriate reconfiguration of the chromatin structure after fertilisation. Somatic cells have very different chromatin structure to sperm and 'reprogramming' of the transferred nuclei must occur within a few hours of activation of reconstructed embryos. Incomplete or inappropriate reprogramming will lead to dysregulation of gene expression and failure of the embryo or foetus to develop normally or to non-fatal developmental abnormalities in those that survive.

Improving success rates is not going to be easy. At present, the only way to assess the 'quality' of embryos is to look at them under the microscope and it is clear that the large majority of embryos that are classified as 'normal' do not develop properly after they have been implanted. A substantial effort is now being made to identify systematic ways of improving reprogramming. One focus is on known mechanisms involved in early development, and in particular on the 'imprinting' of genes. Another is to use technological advances in genomics to screen the expression patterns of tens of thousands of genes to identify differences between the development of 'reconstructed embryos' and those produced by in-vivo or in-vitro fertilisation.

Limitations of nuclear transfer

It is important to recognise the limitations of nuclear transfer. Plans to clone extinct species have attracted a lot of publicity. One Australian project aims to resurrect the 'Tasmanian tiger' by cloning from a specimen that had been preserved in a bottle of alcohol for 153 years and another research group announced plans to clone a mammoth from 20,000-year-old tissue found in the Siberian permafrost. However, the DNA in such samples is hopelessly fragmented and there is no chance of reconstructing a complete genome. In any case, nuclear transfer requires an intact nucleus, with functioning chromosomes. DNA on its own is not enough: many forget that *Jurassic Park* was a work of fiction.

Other obvious requirements for cloning are an appropriate supply of oocytes and surrogate mothers to carry the cloned embryos to term. Cloning of endangered breeds will be possible by using eggs and surrogates from more common breeds of the same species. It may be possible to clone using a closely related species but the chance of successfully carrying a pregnancy to term would be increasingly unlikely if eggs and surrogate mothers are from more distantly related species. Proposals to 'save' the panda by cloning, for example, would seem to have little or no chance of success because it has no close relatives to supply eggs or carry the cloned embryos.

Method of nuclear transfer in livestock

Applications

Nuclear transfer can be viewed in two ways: as a means to create identical copies of animals or as a means of converting cells in culture to live animals. The former has applications in livestock production, the latter provides for the first time an ability to introduce precise genetic modifications into farm animal species.

• *Cloning in farm animal production*
Nuclear transfer can in principle be used to create an infinite number of clones of the very best farm animals. In practice, cloning would be limited to cattle and pigs because it is only in these species that the benefits might justify the costs. Cloned elite cows have already been sold at auction for over $40,000 each in the US but these prices reflect their novelty value rather than their economic worth. To be effective, cloning would have to be integrated systematically into breeding programmes and care would be needed to preserve genetic diversity. It would also remain to be shown that clones do consistently deliver the expected commercial performance and are healthy and that the technology can be applied without compromising animal welfare.

• *Production of human therapeutic proteins*
Human proteins are in great demand for the treatment of a variety of diseases. Whereas some can be purified from blood, this is expensive and runs the risk of contamination by AIDS or hepatitis C. Proteins can be produced in human cell culture but costs are very high and output small. Much larger quantities can be produced in bacteria or yeast but the proteins produced can be difficult to purify

and they lack the appropriate post-translational modifications that are needed for efficacy in vivo.

By contrast, human proteins that have appropriate post-translational modifications can be produced in the milk of transgenic sheep, goats and cattle. Output can be as high as 40 g per litre of milk and costs are relatively low. PPL Therapeutics are one of the leaders in this field and their lead product, alpha-1-antitrypsin, is due to enter phase 3 clinical trials for treatment of cystic fibrosis and emphysema in 2001. Nuclear transfer allows human genes to be inserted at specific points in the genome, improving the reliability of their expression, and allows genes to be deleted or substitutes as well as added.

Nuclear transfer is not a new technique. It was first used in 1952 to study early development in frogs and in the 1980s the technique was used to clone cattle and sheep using cells taken directly from early embryos

---

• *Cell based therapies*
Cell transplants are being developed for a wide variety of common diseases, including Parkinson's Disease, heart attack, stroke and diabetes. Transplanted cells are as likely to be rejected as organs but this problem could be avoided if the type of cells needed could be derived from the patients themselves. The cloning of adult animals from a variety of cell types shows that the egg and early embryo have the capability of 'reprogramming' even fully differentiated cells. Understanding more about the mechanisms involved may allow us to find alternative approaches to 'reprogramming' a patient's own cells without creating (and destroying) human embryos.

Ethics

Many ethical and moral concerns have arisen over the potential

applications of the cloning technology. The technology is still in its infancy and in the meantime, society as a whole has time to contemplate which uses of the technology might be acceptable and which would not. The suddenness of the news of the cloning of the first adult animal caught almost all commentators by surprise and some suggested that we should have fully discussed the implications of our work before we started. The public may see science as a series of 'breakthroughs' but in reality progress is much more continuous. Where in the sequence of events that led to Dolly should we have consulted and with whom? It is also impossible to predict all potential applications of a new technology. Most will be beneficial but all technology can be misused in one way or another. The solution is not to regulate the technology itself but how it is applied.

Those concerned that scientists were 'playing at God' seemed to ignore how much mankind has altered the cards that we were originally dealt. Animals were first domesticated about 5000 years ago and selective breeding since has produced modern strains of livestock, plants and pets which are very different from their original progenitors. In medicine, our current life expectancy of well over 70 years is a result of direct intervention in nature, from improved prenatal care, vaccination and use of antibiotics. The human condition is still far from perfect and there is no particular reason now to call a general halt to what most people view as progress.

Roslin believes it has a clear social responsibility to keep the public informed of the results of its research and is a very active participant in the ongoing public debates about cloning, animal experimentation, genetic modification and human stem cell research.

• The above information is from the Roslin Institute's web site which can be found at www.roslin.ac.uk Alternatively see page 41 for their address details.
© 2000 Roslin Institute

Cloning 'has to do better on animal welfare'

By Robert Uhlig, Technology Correspondent

The scientist who cloned Dolly the Sheep said yesterday that cloning companies are moving ahead too fast without considering the full implications for animal welfare or the safety of food produced from cloned cattle.

American cloning companies are busy making multiple copies of prize breeding cows. They claim that cloning could soon become an economic and routine way of producing dairy and meat animals at a fraction of their market value.

But Ian Wilmut, who led the team that produced Dolly at the Roslin Institute in Edinburgh, told *New Scientist* that the practice should only be sanctioned when cloners had improved their record on animal welfare. 'If companies start marketing this food and there are problems, it will bring the whole technology into disrepute,' he said.

Prof Wilmut said it was vital that large-scale, controlled farm trials of cattle cloning were carried out before any commercial production of cloned meat and dairy food was allowed.

So far, the companies, based largely in America and Japan, have been picking individual prize cows and bulls for cloning rather than conducting farm trials with lots of animals.

Some countries have drawn up guidelines stipulating the circumstances in which commercial farm cloning would be acceptable. In Britain, the Animal Welfare Council said scientists would need to reduce the number of severe pregnancy complications seen in cloning and solve the common problem of cloned calves being born greatly oversized.

However, Prof Wilmut said he believed the companies ought to go further and prove that large-scale farm cloning for food introduced no additional animal welfare problems at all and that clones were just as healthy as ordinary animals. The warning came as scientists continued to find evidence of an increasingly wide range of clone defects.

Jim Robl of the Massachusetts company Hematech said the list included enlarged tongues, squashed faces, bad kidneys, intestinal blockages, immune deficiencies, diabetes and shortened tendons that twisted the feet into useless curves. 'There's no pattern,' he said. 'It's perplexing.'

At the University of Hawaii at Manoa, work on cloned mice suggests that 'all cloned babies have some sort of errors'.

Resurrecting Fido

Britain is officially outlawing human cloning in order to roar ahead with other embryo experiments

By Jerome Burne

A frozen tissue mountain, or at least a sizeable mound, is accumulating in the American west, as grieving pet owners send off scraps of flesh from Fido or Cuddles to be turned into an embryo and stored in liquid nitrogen. Human cloning may be officially outlawed and still the province of fringe cults or maverick researchers, but the promise of pet cloning can be yours on production of a credit card.

After the cloning of laboratory and farm animals, it is the logical next step and potentially an enormously profitable one. There are an estimated 100m cats and dogs in North America and about 10% die every year. You only need a tiny percentage of owners, rich and/or desperate enough to yearn to recreate those happier days, to generate a sizeable industry.

Already there are several web-based firms, such as Canine Cryo-bank, who will sent you a tissue or blood harvesting kit for about $200 and then charge you another $300 or $400 to turn that into embryos. (Handy tip: if a much loved pet dies before you can take a sample, don't despair. Providing you keep the body in the fridge, but not frozen, tissue will remain viable for up to seven days.)

DNA from the tissue is then inserted into a denucleated egg, probably taken from a spayed bitch, and allowed to divide until there is a clutch of embryonic cells, which are then frozen. You then pay 100 or so dollars a year for storage until the biotech breakthrough, always just around the corner, that will allow cloning to take place on an industrial scale. As yet no one has officially cloned a pet, but theoretical prices go from $25,000, through $250,000 to $1m.

Breakthroughs aside, the immediate success of pet cloning depends on papering over an image problem, not unlike the one facing chocolate manufacturers at the moment. The hard sell concentrates on two scenes: sad loss of faithful companion followed by joyous resurrection. What that ignores is life on the embryo plantations. Literally dozens of largely nameless and unloved bitches will be indentured to a lifetime of medical interventions in order to bring Fido back.

Cloning is a terribly wasteful technique. More than 277 embryos were implanted before Dolly the sheep emerged. The rest fell at one of the many hurdles, and cloning dogs, because of their physiology, is much harder. At Texas A&M University, a leading cloning centre, 60 bitches were used to try, unsuccessfully, to clone a single dog – Missy, belonging to an anonymous benefactor who had donated $2.3m to the university in 1998.

The toll on the worker dogs comes firstly from having their ovaries harvested by cutting open the stomach and sucking them out with a glass pipette. Then further operations are necessary to implant the fertilised eggs, which mostly result in miscarriages or still births. The large number of worker dogs are needed because once a de-nucleated egg and the pet's DNA have fused and started dividing, it can't be stored but must be implanted immediately into a receptive female. However, while sheep have a regular fertility cycle of 18 days, dogs ovulate twice a year at random. So you need the numbers to have any chance of finding an ovulating bitch.

But even if the hit rate can be improved, and research scientists are eternally optimistic especially where funding is involved, a new problem is emerging that means the re-incarnated Rover may not be quite what you expected. Evidence is now coming in that successful clones are prey to a much higher incidence of genetic problems, some of which don't emerge until quite late in life. One researcher in Hawaii, for instance, has reported that a proportion of cloned mice develop severe obesity problems at a human-equivalent age of about 30. Cloned cows are often born with enlarged hearts or lungs that do not develop properly. Several scientists think that these problems are inherent in cloning. When the egg re-

programmes the donor's DNA so that it returns to its embryonic state, it's doing in a few hours something that normally takes months or years as sperm and eggs develop. The result is random genetic errors.

While some pet owners' sentimentality may be sufficiently selective to ignore the toll on other animals taken by cloning, the possibility that resurrected Fido will blow up like a balloon some years down the line will be far harder to overlook. If the commercial cloners have to start indemnifying themselves against such potential disasters, the whole project may look distinctly less attractive.

One idea about pet cloning is that it is part of a hidden agenda. It is a way of softening us up for human cloning. It domesticates the process, so that once you have cloned a much loved labrador, doing the same for another family member won't seem so alien. That certainly seems to be the message of an extraordinary web site, launched earlier this month. CloneConsult promises to provide a clone of a medium weight pet – 10lb to 99lb – for $1m and a human clone for $2m, both to be delivered within two years. The options even have shopping baskets above them and they do, of course, take credit cards.

On the other hand pet cloning, once its realities sink in, may finish off the whole oversold notion of human cloning once and for all. Then when they pull the plug on the frozen tissue, it can probably be recycled into pet food.

• The above article first appeared in the *Guardian* Newspaper.

© *Jerome Burne*

The unclonables

By Andy Coghlan

It's safe to clone primates, including humans, but not mice, rats, sheep, cows, pigs and opossums, claim geneticists. They says there is a vital genetic difference separating the clonables from the unclonables.

'It lays to rest some of the technical worries about cloning,' says Randy Jirtle of Duke University in Durham, North Carolina. But other researchers say the claims are dangerous.

'The authors have allowed themselves to over-interpret their interesting results,' says Ian Wilmut, creator of Dolly the sheep. 'I hope that this will not be used to give encouragement to those who wish to clone humans.'

Cloning often fails because of 'large offspring syndrome', in which animals grow too big in the womb and often die at birth. Jirtle and his colleagues say this is because a gene called IGF2R that slows growth can get switched off.

In most mammals, including all those cloned so far, the paternal copy of IGF2R is 'mothballed' in a process known as imprinting. If the remaining maternal copy is accidentally switched off during cloning, nothing prevents large offspring syndrome.

After analysing tissue from an array of mammals, Jirtle found that in primates neither copy of IGF2R is imprinted – or imprintable. 'We've got two brakes, whereas most cloned animals have one, and our brakes can't be altered,' he says.

'But to say this makes cloning safer is a ludicrous claim,' says Robin Lovell-Badge, a cloning specialist at the National Institute for Medical Research in London. Disruption of other imprinted genes might be just as important, he says.

• From *New Scientist* 25 August 2001.

© *Copyright Reed Business Information Ltd*

Black and white, not bred all over

Sanjida O'Connell reports on plans to clone pandas to save them from extinction

Just over two years ago, China announced it was going to clone the giant panda, the country's national symbol.

Pandas are extremely endangered; there are only 1,000 left in the wild and a hundred in captivity. The move to begin cloning the animal was prompted by unsuccessful attempts to increase its population using in-vitro fertilisation and artificial insemination.

Pandas are notorious for their feeble efforts when it comes to mating. Even in the wild, where their sex drive may be higher, the survival rate of the cubs is very low: more than half of them die shortly after birth.

Unusually, this summer six panda cubs were born in the Wolong Giant Panda Reserves in the south-west province of Sichuan, in China. However, zoologists were reluctant to join in the celebrations: it is widely held that the panda will become extinct within 10 years. Three years ago, researchers at the Cheng Du Zoo and the biology department of the United University of Sichuan successfully cloned a gene linked to a nervous disorder, one which commonly leads to death in giant pandas. A year later, Dr Chen Dayuan, from China's Academy of Sciences, began a research programme aimed at cloning a panda.

Dayuan took the nucleus from the cell of an adult panda (this is the part of the cell that contains all the genetic material) and inserted it into an egg from a rabbit which had had its nucleus removed, to produce a ball of cells that could become a panda embryo.

So far this step has proved successful. The difficulty will be growing a panda out of a collection of cells. Dayuan is currently looking for suitable surrogate mothers and is considering black and sloth bears as candidates. Dayuan hopes to have a panda clone within the next five years.

Not everyone in China is in favour of trying to clone the panda. One of the country's leading panda experts, Dr Pan Wenshi, has studied them in the wild for two decades. He believes that attempts to clone this rare animal will detract from efforts to preserve the species in the wild.

> *Pandas are notorious for their feeble efforts when it comes to mating. Even in the wild, the survival rate of the cubs is very low: more than half of them die shortly after birth*

He has also dismissed the widely accepted theory that the panda's threatened extinction is due to its decline in fertility. He argues that the main reason pandas are an endangered species is because humans have decimated their habitat.

Meanwhile, in Australia, attempts to clone an extinct species, the Tasmanian tiger, have begun. This is not a cat at all, but rather a wolf-like marsupial wiped out by British settlers, who blamed them for killing sheep and other farm animals. A bounty was even put on the animal's head in 1888. As a result, the last Tasmanian tiger died in a zoo in 1936.

The great white hope of the Australian Museum in Sydney is a six-month-old Tasmanian tiger pup preserved in alcohol since 1866. Researchers have already extracted samples from the dead animal's heart, liver, muscles and bone marrow. These DNA samples, approximately 2,000 bases long, will be used to create a genetic library. Its genes will then be inserted into the egg of a close relative, probably the Tasmanian devil or the numbat, another marsupial.

Dr Don Colgan, head of the evolutionary biology department of the Australian Museum, believes that it could take 10 to 15 years before the tiger is successfully cloned. Other scientists are sceptical whether the project will work at all, or whether it should even be carried out.

'This is just boys playing with genetic toys,' says Michael Lynch, manager of the Tasmanian Conservation Trust in Hobart. 'We could better take that money and put it into saving the species we humans are driving to extinction every year,' he adds.

However, Colgan argues that his team's research will create new scientific breakthroughs that will help conservation efforts in other species.

'From an evolutionary biologist's point of view, we should be looking at the longer term, such as 200 to 300 years ahead,' Colgan says. 'And this whole research area is where you should be looking if you really want to save species.'

• The above article first appeared in the *Guardian* Newspaper.

© Sanjida O'Connell

WE ARE GOING TO SAVE THE PANDA BY CLONING – – ITS HABITAT!

Clone farm

Billions of identical chickens could soon be rolling off production lines

By Andrea Graves

Factory farming could soon enter a new era of mass production. Companies in the US are developing the technology needed to 'clone' chickens on a massive scale.

Once a chicken with desirable traits has been bred or genetically engineered, tens of thousands of eggs, which will hatch into identical copies, could roll off the production lines every hour. Billions of clones could be produced each year to supply chicken farms with birds that all grow at the same rate, have the same amount of meat and taste the same.

This, at least, is the vision of the US's National Institute of Science and Technology, which has given Origen Therapeutics of Burlingame, California, and Embrex of North Carolina $4.7 million to help fund research. The prospect has alarmed animal welfare groups, who fear it could increase the suffering of farm birds.

That's unlikely to put off the poultry industry, however, which wants disease-resistant birds that grow faster on less food. 'Producers would like the same meat quantity but to use reduced inputs to get there,' says Mike Fitzgerald of Origen.

To meet this demand, Origen aims to 'create an animal that is effectively a clone', he says. Normal cloning doesn't work in birds because eggs can't be removed and implanted. Instead, the company is trying to bulk-grow embryonic stem cells taken from fertilised eggs as soon as they're laid. 'The trick is to culture the cells without them starting to differentiate, so they remain pluripotent,' says Fitzgerald.

Using a long-established technique, these donor cells will then be injected into the embryo of a freshly laid, fertilised recipient egg, forming a chick that is a 'chimera'. Strictly speaking a chimera isn't a clone, because it contains cells from both donor and recipient. But Fitzgerald says it will be enough if, say, 95 per cent of a chicken's body develops from donor cells. 'In the poultry world, it doesn't matter if it's not 100 per cent,' he says.

Cloning chickens

With its patent still at application stage, Origen is unwilling to reveal if it can reliably obtain such chimeras. But it has occasionally created the ideal: chicks that are 100 per cent donor-derived, or pure clones.

Another challenge for Origen

> *Billions of clones could be produced each year to supply chicken farms with birds that all grow at the same rate, have the same amount of meat and taste the same*

is to scale up production. To do this, it has teamed up with Embrex, which produces machines that can inject vaccines into up to 50,000 eggs an hour. Embrex is now trying to modify the machines to locate the embryo and inject the cells into precisely the right spot without killing it. Automating the process will be tricky, admits Nandini Mandu of Embrex. Even when it's done by hand, up to 75 per cent of the embryos die.

In future, Origen envisages freezing stem cells from different strains of chicken. If orders come in for a particular strain, millions of eggs could be produced in months or even weeks. At present, maintaining all the varieties the market might call for is too expensive for breeders, and it takes years to breed enough chickens to produce the billions of eggs that farmers need.

Fitzgerald insists that genetic modification isn't on Origen's menu. The stem cells will come from eggs laid by unmodified pedigree birds, he says. All the same, Origen's website says the company has

licences for tools for genetically engineering birds, and it talks about engineering birds that lay eggs containing medical drugs.

Animal welfare groups say that it would be cruel if breeders used the technology to mass-produce the fastest-growing birds. Some birds already go lame when bone growth doesn't keep pace with muscle growth. 'The last thing they should be doing is increasing growth rates,' says Abigail Hall of Britain's Royal Society for the Prevention of Cruelty to Animals.

There are other dangers. If one bird were vulnerable to a disease, all its clones would be too. But if one set of clones fell victim to a disease, the technology would allow farmers to 'roll out' a resistant set rapidly.

There could also be benefits for consumers, as farmers could quickly adopt strains that don't carry food-poisoning bacteria such as Salmonella, for instance. Whether shoppers will buy meat from a clone, even if it's not genetically engineered, remains to be seen. And the FDA has yet to decide whether meat and milk from cloned animals is fit for humans.

• From *New Scientist* 18 August 2001.
©*Reed Business Information Ltd*

Genetic engineering campaign

Information from the Compassion in World Farming Trust (CIWF)

What is farm animal genetic engineering?

Scientists and biotechnology companies want to use genetic engineering to produce farm animals designed to be more productive in some way, such as having larger muscles (being meatier), being faster-growing or producing more milk and wool. At the moment several pharmaceutical companies are also aiming to produce herds of transgenic animals carrying human genes, to produce human proteins in their milk for human use. They also hope to use 'humanised' pigs to provide spare-part organs for transplants to people (xenotransplants).

Why are farm animals cloned?

Cloning is the production of a precise genetic copy of an animal, a human or a plant, or of some part of them. The first farm animal cloning experiments at the Roslin Institute in Scotland in 1996 and 1997 all involved methods where the genetic material (DNA) is removed from a cell of one animal (the one the scientists want to clone) and put into the egg-cell of another animal. The genetic material can also be genetically engineered to introduce some new trait, before it is transferred to the egg-cell. The resulting embryo is then placed in the oviduct of a 'surrogate' mother animal for a short time to start its development and is then transferred yet again to the 'surrogate' mother ewe who will give birth. Because genetic engineering is such a hit-and-miss technology and produces so few 'successes' many scientists see cloning as a way of rapidly multiplying the few 'successful' transgenic animals. A lot of biotechnology companies now see this as the best way to get a herd of identical genetically engineered animals for commercial use or for use in xenotransplantation.

What are the welfare problems in genetic engineering of farm animals?

CIWF believes that genetic engineering and cloning experiments (and their commercial use) are a very serious threat to the welfare of farm animals. Genetic engineering of animals is a hit-or-miss process. A large number of animals have to be subjected to surgery and often death in order to produce a few 'successes'. Only a small percentage of the animals used in experiments 'express' the foreign DNA and even if they do, the results may be far from intended. The 'Beltsville Pigs' produced in the USA in the 1980s with foreign genes to make them grow quicker suffered from degenerative joint disease (they

Even if cloning becomes more efficient, CIWF believes it is likely to be a welfare disaster for farm animals

couldn't stand up), gastric ulceration and other problems. It is likely that experiments going on now often have similar disastrous results, but the scientists do not always reveal the full details of their 'failures'.

In cloning experiments, the scientists admit there are large losses of embryos and serious congenital malformations in many animals, which may be born missing organs or greatly oversized. The UK's Farm Animal Welfare Council said in 1990 that cloning should not be allowed commercially while these problems still continue.

Even if cloning becomes more efficient, CIWF believes it is likely to be a welfare disaster for farm animals. Selective breeding has had a bad record for welfare. Herds of identical cloned animals would lead to even greater loss of genetic diversity with unforeseeable results in terms of illness for the animals. Transgenic pigs used for xenotransplants would have to live their lives in unnatural, sterile conditions. CIWF believes that the suffering involved in cloning and genetically engineering cannot be justified by the benefits claimed by the scientists and multinational biotechnology companies.

• The above information is an extract from the Compassion in World Farming Trust's web site which can be found at www.ciwf.org.uk
© *Compassion in World Farming Trust (CIWF)*

ADDITIONAL RESOURCES

You might like to contact the following organisations for further information. Due to the increasing cost of postage, many organisations cannot respond to enquiries unless they receive a stamped, addressed envelope.

Advocates for Animals
10 Queensferry Street
Edinburgh, EH2 4PG
Tel: 0131 225 6039
Fax: 0131 220 6377
Web site:
www.advocatesforanimals.org.uk
Protects animals from cruelty and prevents the infliction of suffering.

The British Union for the Abolition of Vivisection (BUAV)
16a Crane Grove
London, N7 8NN
Tel: 020 7700 4888
Fax: 020 7700 0252
E-mail: info@buav.org
Web site: www.buav.org
The BUAV believes animals are entitled to respect and compassion which animal experiments deny them.

CARE (Christian Action Research and Education)
53 Romney Street
London, SW1P 3RF
Tel: 020 7233 0455
Fax: 020 7233 0983
E-mail: info@care.org.uk
Web site: www.care.org.uk
Produces publications presenting a Christian perspective on moral issues.

Centre for Bioethics and Public Policy (CBPP)
51 Romney Street
London, SW1 3RF
Tel: 020 7227 4706
Fax: 020 7233 0983
E-mail: info@cbpp.ac.uk
Web site: www.cbpp.ac.uk
Focuses on the relations of bioethics and public policy, including issues such as Euthanasia and Cloning.

The Christian Institute
26 Jesmond Road
Newcastle Upon Tyne, NE2 4PQ
Tel: 0191 281 5664
Fax: 0191 281 4272
E-mail: info@christian.org.uk
Web site: www.christian.org.uk
The Christian Institute is concerned with the family, education and pro-life issues and religious liberties.

Compassion in World Farming Trust (CIWF)
Charles House, 5a Charles Street
Petersfield, GU32 3EH
Tel: 01730 268070
Fax: 01730 260791
E-mail: ciwftrust@ciwf.co.uk
Web site: www.ciwf.co.uk
Compassion in World Farming has been campaigning for improvements in the welfare of farm animals for the last thirty years.

Dr Hadwen Trust for Humane Research
84a Tilehouse Street
Hitchin, SG5 2HY
Tel: 01462 436819
Fax: 01462 436844
E-mail: info@drhadwentrust.org.uk
Web site: www.drhadwentrust.org.uk
Funds non-animal research into major health problems such as cancer and heart disease.

Human Genetics Alert
Unit 112, Aberdeen House
22-24 Highbury Grove
London, N5 2EA
Tel: 020 7704 6100
E-mail: info@hgalert.org
Web site: www.hgalert.org
Addresses the ethical, social and political problems raised in human genetics.

LIFE
LIFE House, Newbold Terrace
Leamington Spa
Warwickshire, CV32 4EA
Tel: 01926 421587
Fax: 01926 336497
E-mail: info@lifeuk.org
Web site: www.lifeuk.org
Upholds the utmost respect for human life from fertilisation onwards.

Medical Research Council (MRC)
20 Park Crescent
London, W1B 1AL
Tel: 020 7636 5422
Fax: 020 7436 6179
Web site: www.mrc.ac.uk
The MRC aims to improve health by promoting research into all areas of medical and related science.

ProLife Alliance
PO Box 13395
London, SW3 6XE
Tel: 020 7351 9955
Fax: 020 7349 0450
E-mail: info@prolife.org.uk
Web site: www.prolife.org.uk
Seeks to ensure the right to life of all, the most basic and fundamental human right.

Research Defence Society (RDS)
58 Great Marlborough Street
London, W1F 7JY
Tel: 020 7287 2818
Fax: 020 7287 2627
Web site: www.rds-online.org.uk
Represents medical researchers in the public debate about the use of animals in medical research and testing.

Roslin Institute
Roslin BioCentre
Midlothian, Scotland, EH25 9PS
Tel: 0131 527 4200
Fax: 0131 440 0434
E-mail: roslin.library@bbsrc.ac.uk
Web site: www.roslin.ac.uk
Roslin Institute is one of the world's leading centres for research on farm and other animals.

Society, Religion and Technology Project
John Knox House, 45 High Street
Edinburgh, EH1 1SR
Tel: 0131 556 2953
Fax: 0131 556 7478
E-mail: srtp@srtp.org.uk
Web site: www.srtp.org.uk
Works to foster an informed understanding in society of the issues of current and future technologies.

The Wellcome Trust
The Wellcome Building
183 Euston Road
London, NW1 2BE
Tel: 020 7611 8888
Fax: 020 7611 8545
E-mail: contact@wellcome.ac.uk
Web site: www.wellcome.ac.uk
Works to foster and promote research with the aim of improving human and animal health.

INDEX

ACKNOWLEDGEMENTS

The publisher is grateful for permission to reproduce the following material.

While every care has been taken to trace and acknowledge copyright, the publisher tenders its apology for any accidental infringement or where copyright has proved untraceable. The publisher would be pleased to come to a suitable arrangement in any such case with the rightful owner.

Chapter One: Human Cloning

Human cloning, © Guardian Newspapers Limited 2001, *Cloning timeline*, © LIFE, *Human cloning*, © The Christian Institute, *Public perspectives on human cloning*, © The Wellcome Trust, *Attitudes of the general public*, © MORI (Market & Opinion Research International Limited), *Cloning: disaster or necessity?*, © Guardian Newspapers Limited 2001, *Cloning*, © Centre for Bioethics and Public Policy (CBPP), *Birth of a miracle*, © Reed Business Information Ltd., *Team prepares to clone human being*, © Guardian Newspapers Limited, *Human cloning*, © ProLife Alliance, *Cloned babies*, © Church of Scotland Society, Religion and Technology Project, *Stars are offered way to stop fans cloning them*, © Telegraph Group Limited, London 2001, *The benefits of human cloning*, © Human Cloning Foundation, *To clone or not to clone?*, © CARE (Christian Action Research and Education), *Who wants to clone?*, © LIFE, *Reproductive and 'therapeutic' cloning*, © Comment on Reproductive Ethics (CORE), *World ban 'the only way to stop baby cloning'*, © Telegraph Group Limited, London 2001, *Are embryonic stem cells a step too far?*, © Church of Scotland Society, Religion and Technology Project, *Stem cell therapy*, © Medical Research Council (MRC), *Briefing on non-reproductive cloning*, © Human Genetics Alert, *International moratorium on human cloning*, © The Royal Society, *Scientists boycott 'human clone' conference*, © Telegraph Group Limited, London 2001, *Cloning – the fountain of youth and never-ending drugs*, © Advocates for Animals.

Chapter Two: Animal Cloning

Animal cloning, © Research Defence Society (RDS), *Attitudes towards life sciences*, © MORI (Market & Opinion Research International Limited), *Ethical aspects of animal cloning*, © Dr Hadwen Trust for Humane Research, *Cloning*, © BUAV, *Technique*, © BUAV, *Cloning animals*, © The Roslin Institute, *Cloning 'has to do better on animal welfare'*, © Telegraph Group Limited, London 2001, *Resurrecting Fido*, © Jerome Burne, *The unclonables*, © Reed Business Information Ltd., *Black and white, not bred all over*, © Sanjida O'Connell, *Clone farm*, © Reed Business Information Ltd., *Genetic engineering campaign*, © Compassion in World Farming Trust (CIWF).

Photographs and illustrations:

Pages 1, 15, 20, 28, 39: Pumpkin House, pages 10, 13, 16, 18, 24, 26, 31, 38: Simon Kneebone.

Craig Donnellan
Cambridge
January, 2002